Daily Express

YOUR MONEY

How to Make the Most of it

NIKI CHESWORTH

KOGAN
PAGE

First published in 1994

Kogan Page Limited
120 Pentonville Road
London N1 9JN
© Niki Chesworth and Express Newspapers plc, 1994

British Library Cataloguing in Publication Data
A CIP record for this book is available from the British Library.

ISBN 0 7494 1188 0

Typeset by Saxon Graphics Ltd, Derby
Printed in England by Clays Ltd, St Ives plc

Contents

Strength, Quality, Endurance.

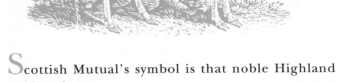

Scottish Mutual's symbol is that noble Highland resident the stag.

It is an appropriate symbol, because like the stag we offer qualities of strength and endurance.

We employ no direct sales people. We believe that pensions, investment and life assurance are so important that members of the public should only part with their money on the expert advice of an independent financial adviser, who is bound to recommend a suitable policy from the whole marketplace.

If you do not have an independent financial adviser (IFA), you can call IFA Promotion on 0483 461461 for details of IFAs in your area.

Scottish Mutual Assurance plc

Registered in Scotland no. 133846.
Registered Office: 109 St Vincent Street, Glasgow G2 5HN.
A Member of LAUTRO.

Acknowledgements

A large number of people have very generously helped in the preparation of this book. In particular I would like to thank Pauline Hedges of the British Bankers' Association, the Halifax Building Society, Legal & General, Royal Insurance and Chase de Vere.

I would also like to thank my husband, Stephen Chesworth, for helping to type and research the many pages of this book. And thanks also the many readers of the Daily Express who have written in asking for information and advice from the Money desk over the years. This book aims to answer some of the questions that they have asked.

Have we got plans for you!

After 18 years of knowing the UK market inside-out, Albany Life have the quality products that can cover all aspects of business life. We are a leading unit-linked life assurance company offering competitive life assurance cover, savings and investments plans and pensions. We also provide advice on inheritance planning, business assurance and personal investment and pension planning. Albany Life Investment funds are managed by Mercury Asset Management PLC – Europe's largest pension fund managers. And are owned by Met Life, one of the world's largest insurance organisations, a company with over £80 billion worth of assets under management. It's because we're secure that you are. Call FREEPHONE ALBANY to obtain more information.

Albany Life

✿ **A Metropolitan Life Company**

HAVE YOU THOUGHT ABOUT YOUR FINANCIAL AFFAIRS RECENTLY?

Thought about:-

- ❑ **Investment -** which suits you best?
- ❑ **Regular Savings -** how nice it would be to accumulate a lump sum.
- ❑ **School Fees -** how quickly the years pass and how expensive it all seems.
- ❑ **Pension Planning -** how will you cope on a reduced income in retirement?
- ❑ **Inheritance Tax -** how will you protect your family?

You do not have to become one of the world's great thinkers to get your financial affairs under control -

LET GODWINS HELP YOU.

We have been providing financial advice to our clients for over 50 years and are recognised as being amongst the leading specialists in this field in the UK.

We are independent which means that we are not tied to any life assurance company or other financial institution.

With Godwins you can be sure that you are getting truly impartial advice - a service which we can provide nationwide through our 27 offices.

You may think that financial matters are too confusing -

WE KNOW THAT WE CAN HELP.

For further details please telephone Mark Chandler on 0252 544484 or write to Mark Chandler, Godwins Limited, FREEPOST, Farnborough, Hampshire GU14 7BR - No stamp required.

GODWINS LIMITED IS A MEMBER OF IMRO   An **AON** Company

Introduction

Money is a problem for most people. But it doesn't have to be. It is up to you to run your finances, instead of letting your finances rule your life. However, it is not easy to take control.

The world of finance is increasingly complex. There are so many choices to make. The days when a bank account was just a bank account are over. There are now dozens of different types, from those that pay interest to those that give free overdrafts. At one time homebuyers were grateful to be offered a mortgage. Now there are hundreds of different homeloans to choose from.

Then there is the problem of trying to get the best insurance deal, a good rate of interest on your savings, the right pension scheme and enough life cover to protect your family.

It is easy to be ripped off. You could end up losing hundreds if not thousands of pounds by picking the wrong investment, mortgage or insurance product.

However, it is not easy to get the best deal. Money is very confusing. Although financial companies have made great efforts to simplify their literature, most people are still bemused by the plethora of financial jargon. In an age when we are used to reading the labels on our food, most people still do not read the small print on their insurance or investment policies, let alone check their bank statements. Even if you do read the small print, the chances are you may not understand all of it and even if you do, how will you know if it is a good deal or not?

The obvious solution is to seek advice. But where do you go, and how do you know what questions to ask or whether the advice you are getting is good?

This book is designed to answer these questions in a concise, simple and easy-to-understand form. Jargon is kept to the minimum and where used it is explained. The book takes you through everything you need to know to make the most of your money, from day-to-day budgeting to more advanced financial planning and investment, so that you can be in control of your finances and more confident when dealing with your money.

I hope you will find it a worthwhile investment and at the end will be not only wiser but richer.

The Daily Express Guides

The Daily Express and Kogan Page have joined forces to publish a series of practical guides offering no-nonsense advice on a wide range of financial, legal and business topics.

Whether you want to manage your money better, make more money, get a new business idea off the ground – and make sure it's legal – there's a Daily Express Guide for you.

Titles published so far are:

Great Ideas for Making Money
Niki Chesworth

Your Money
How to Make the Most of it
Niki Chesworth

You and the Law
A Simple Guide to All Your Legal Problems
Susan Singleton

How to Cut Your Tax Bill Without Breaking the Law
Grant Thornton, Chartered Accountants

Be Your Own Boss
How to Set Up a Successful Small Business
David McMullan

Readymade Business Letters That Get Results
Jim Douglas

Available from all good bookshops, or to obtain further information please contact the publishers at the address below:

Kogan Page Ltd
120 Pentonville Rd
LONDON N1 9JN
Tel: 071-278 0433
Fax: 071-837 6348

1

Making the most of your money

Consider how much effort you put into earning money and how little you put into looking after it.

If you work 35 hours a week for 48 weeks a year for 40 years, then you will have spent over 67,000 hours earning a living. Compare that with how much time you spend looking after your money. You will probably spend more time dreaming about having more wealth, more days spending your hard-earned cash and more hours arguing over money matters than you do on financial planning. Yet failure to manage your money can cost you dearly.

You are probably giving away some of it, without even knowing. Some 30 million people are paying too much tax. If they sorted out their financial affairs, they could save a staggering £8 billion a year.

There is also £10 billion in unclaimed premium bond prizes and millions in 'lost' bank balances and unclaimed life insurance policies. Savers are losing another £1 billion a year on money languishing in accounts that pay poor rates of interest.

Five million savers and investors are paying tax on their nest eggs — even though they don't have to. That's another £480 million down the drain. Billions of pounds more are wasted in unnecessary interest payments, overpayment of bills, bank charges that should be avoided and poor investments.

When it comes to picking a mortgage, savings or bank account, credit card, loan or investment plan, very few people shop around to make sure they are getting the best deal.

More time and thought usually goes into picking a new car or dress than selecting a life policy. And most people spend longer each year planning their two-week summer holiday than they do planning their retirement — even though this could last for 20 years.

But time spent on your money is time worth spending.

Consider the following. Mr A and Mr B bought semis next door to each other 25 years ago. They were the same age (29 at the time), both took out an endowment mortgage and both paid £30 into their endowment every month.

However, they did not pick the same life insurance company. As a result, Mr A is now receiving a cheque for £20,500 more than his neighbour Mr B. This figure is the difference between the best and worst paying endowment policies over the past 25 years.

Getting your finances in order

If you needed to make an insurance claim, would you know what your policy number is, or where to find it? And what if you wanted to sell your shares? Could you lay your hands on your share certificate?

Most people know vaguely where their paperwork is kept, but in the event of a fire how would you cope if all your documents were lost?

To keep track of your finances you need to be organised and the best way to achieve that is to set up a filing system. Always keep copies of documents, from tax returns to bank statements.

Then you need to make a note of vital information, so that should the worst come to the worst there is a record of key contacts and numbers. This list should be kept in a safe place, which could be your bank safety deposit along with any vital documents such as wills and insurance policy documents (but check out the fee first). Always keep a copy of the list yourself — even banks can burn down!

Making the list will also help to concentrate your mind and encourage you to look after your vital documents. Here is a list of the essentials:

- national insurance and tax numbers;
- passport number;
- payroll number;
- bank branch and account numbers;
- credit card numbers;
- building society accounts;
- life assurance policy details;

- motor insurance policy and 24-hour hotline number;
- mortgage lender and account number;
- pension details;
- household policy number and helpline details;
- where your will is kept.

Learning how to budget

Charles Dickens' Mr Micawber, in *David Copperfield*, defined happiness as a balanced budget. He said: 'Annual income twenty pounds, annual expenditure nineteen nineteen six, result happiness. Annual income twenty pounds, annual expenditure twenty pounds ought and six, result misery.'

Budgeting can be one of the hardest disciplines to undertake, particularly if money is tight. It will depend on your plans and priorities. Before you can decide what you want to spend, have to spend or need to save, you have to assess all your finances.

First you should weigh up your income against your expenditure. Start by keeping a record of what you spend on a weekly or monthly basis. This will concentrate your mind and highlight where you are wasting money and where you can make savings.

Then draw up your expenditure budget. To be on the safe side, add at least a ten per cent contingency for unforeseen problems. Allow for indulgences and more expensive times of the year, such as school holidays or the winter months when heating bills are higher and Christmas presents must be bought.

TABLE 1 Expenditure

Rent/mortgage	_____
Food bills	_____
Clothes/shoes	_____
House contents insurance	_____
Life insurance/endowments	_____
Pensions	_____
Gas	_____
Electricity	_____
Water rates	_____
Council tax	_____
Telephone	_____
TV licence	_____

Travel costs _____
Petrol _____
Car tax, insurance and MOT _____
Car breakdown insurance _____
Catalogue/credit card/loan payments _____
Toiletries _____
Dry cleaning/laundry _____
Club memberships _____
Hairdressing _____
Snacks/sweets/cigarettes _____
Newspapers/books/magazines _____
Children's pocket/dinner money _____
Daily milk _____
School/college fees/books/uniforms _____
Window cleaner/gardener/cleaning lady _____
Nanny/au pair/childminder _____
Medical/dental/optical care _____
Holidays _____
Replacements — washing machines etc _____
Bank charges/overdraft interest _____
Incidentals _____
Other _____

TOTAL _____

Work out all bills on your balance sheet on a monthly basis. For example for your car tax divide the annual cost by 12 and for clothes and shoes work out an average. Don't forget to include all items of essential expenditure. Then allow extra for emergencies. If you don't you will blow your budget if the toaster explodes and you need to replace it.

Some outgoings are obviously monthly, like mortgage or rent, while others which are normally annual, biannual or quarterly can be paid monthly through a budget plan — like the telephone, gas, electricity, council tax, car insurance and household insurance. Water bills are usually paid twice a year.

Then work out your income on a monthly basis and fill in the table below:

TABLE 2 Income

Take-home pay	_____
Pension income	_____
Savings and investment interest	_____
Other income such as rent	_____
TOTAL	_____

Finally, take your income away from your expenditure to find out if you are solvent. If you are not then work out ways to cut your expenditure or increase your earnings.

Balancing the budget

It is usually far easier to shed expenditure than put on income. But you should consider ways of increasing your income, while reducing your expenditure:

- *Overtime* This may not be an option (particularly during the current recession) but if it is on offer or you can ask to do extra hours for extra pay, go for it. (But remember, if it is going to cost you an extra £2 to get home and that is all you are going to get after tax, it may not make financial sense.)
- *Part-time work* If you put in a few extra hours after work or at weekends you can not only pull in extra cash but also cut down on the amount of time in which you can spend money!
- *Job change* Again, this is not easy. If you see a better-paid job, do consider it. (But don't forget to weigh up job security against extra earnings.)
- *Make the most of your assets* If you have a spare room then why not rent it out? Under the Government's rent-a-room scheme you can get up to £65 a week in rent tax free.

Expenditure tips

If overspending is your problem, set yourself a target to cut your outgoings and try to stick to it. This is the only way to achieve your aims. Here are some useful tips:

- *Fuel bills* Turn your central heating off in the late spring and summer and for the rest of the year turn your thermostat down one degree (saving between £17.50 and £47 a year) and wear a woolly jumper instead. Don't forget to turn off the lights when you are not in a room and watch out for the costs of running appliances such as televisions, videos and cookers that are left permanently switched on — they can cost up to £40 a year to run. Lag water tanks and pipes and save £30 a year by fitting loft insulation.

- *Telephones* Only make phone calls in the evenings and at weekends. If you must call at other times, keep your calls as short as possible.
- *Travel* Try to travel when you can get cheap day returns. Make the most of season ticket rates. And if you drive to work, why not share your car — and the costs — with a colleague or friend.
- *Insurance* This is likely to be a major household bill. Shop around for your car, household and contents insurance and you could cut your bills in half.
- *Food* Shopping around for your food can also save you pounds. Think of all the food that is wasted and don't overstock your larder.
- *Finance costs* You could cut your mortgage bills by shopping around. The cost of bank loans and credit card bills can also be slashed with careful planning.
- *Think twice* before getting out your purse or cheque book. Think twice about whether you really need to spend your cash and, if so, whether you are getting the best buy.

Setting yourself targets

Now that you know how your finances stand, you should set yourself goals. These could be to pay off debts and become solvent or more ambitious plans such as buying a new home.

Sit down and decide what you want to achieve, make a note of it and set a deadline. Start to work to short-term goals — when you meet these it will encourage you to continue with your budget plans — and then decide longer-term aims:

1. *Short-term* aim 3–6 months: (eg saving £30 a month or repaying £20 off my debts).
2. *Medium-term* aim 6 months to 2 years: (eg world cruise, new car or buying a flat).
3. *Long-term* aim 2–10 years: (eg retiring early, paying off my mortgage).

Goals are important as they are the reason why you are budgeting and taking control of your finances.

2

Making the most of your current account

Bank and building society accounts

Your current account — whether it is at a bank or building society — is central to your finances. It is the key to making the most of your money. So it should be the first thing you look at when you try to put your finances in shape.

- The golden rules are: avoid bank charges whenever possible; use your bank; take advantage of free banking while it is still on offer; and make sure you are earning a good rate of interest on money sitting in your account.
- Never borrow without the consent of your bank, because the charges are high. It can cost £120 to have an unauthorised overdraft of £60 for a month — in effect twice as much as you were overdrawn. This is money down the drain.
- Over 2.5 million people go overdrawn every year, incurring bank charges that they could avoid with careful financial planning.
- Even those who have money in the bank need to be careful. Make the most of interest if you keep your account in credit. Interest rates are usually pitiful and often hardly worth having. However, by shopping around or switching to a high interest cheque account (which normally requires a higher minimum balance) you can get a far better deal.
- Remember to use your spare cash to pay off borrowings. It is better to pay off debt on which interest is 20 per cent than to borrow and have savings which are earning just a fraction of that rate.
- Ensure that you use banking facilities — such as direct debits, standing orders and cash machines — to best effect so that your

finances run themselves.
- Always check your bank statements and ensure that you have a copy of the bank's tariff of charges.
- To get your finances on the right track, ensure that your salary and other income is paid directly into your bank.

Choosing a bank or building society

Most people open a bank account at their nearest branch, one where a member of their family has an account or a bank recommended by their first place of work. Although gimmicks can sway teenagers and students into opening an account with a particular bank, little thought usually goes into choosing which bank or building society looks after your finances. Yet this is often a lifelong relationship.

You are more likely to change your spouse than change your bank.

Part of this reluctance to switch banks is down to fear (follow the tips later in this chapter to ensure your move is smooth). There is no point in remaining with a bank when the branch near you has been closed and you have to walk miles in your lunch hour just to pay in cash. And if your working hours have changed and you never get a chance to go to the bank without having to take the morning off, why not opt for one with different opening hours or one that allows you to bank by phone?

Choosing which bank or building society to have your bank account with (and there is no reason why you cannot have more than one account or different accounts for different purposes) takes a bit of effort.

Prioritise what is important to you. If you lead a busy life and do not get a chance to go to the bank very often, but need to visit the branch to pay in money, pick a bank that has a branch open near you on a Saturday.

Alternatively, if you want to be able to ring your bank and tell them to pay XYZ amount off your Access or Visa bill or set up a direct debit to pay the electricity bill, then go for a bank that has a telephone banking service open the sort of hours that suit you.

Consider the following and see which you need:

- Branch near your home/work/shops.
- Cash dispensing machine in convenient place, plus link-ups with

other banks and building societies' automatic teller machine (ATM) networks.

- Cash machine that allows you to pay money in.
- Cash machine that gives mini-statements.
- Opening hours — either early mornings or late afternoons or Saturdays.
- Telephone banking service.
- Number of other branches — so if you often travel round the UK you have no problem finding a branch.
- Reputation — you don't want to bank with a future Bank of Credit and Commerce International (BCCI) and lose all your money.
- Personal recommendation — ask your friends, family and colleagues what they think of the bank.
- Speed of service — if you are always in a hurry do not opt for the bank or building society that always has a queue.
- Cheque clearing times — some building societies take longer to clear cheques than banks.

Choosing an account

Again, which account you choose depends on what you want to get out of it.

If you rarely write cheques, only use your bank account for the odd direct debit and are always in credit with at least £1000 in your account, then do not go for the traditional bank account. Opt instead for an interest-bearing current account or a high interest cheque account (known in the banking world as a HICA). However, watch out for poor rates of interest. Even so-called high interest cheque accounts do not always pay top rates.

You may be better off keeping less in your current account and putting your cash in a savings account.

Watch out also for deposit accounts offered by banks. These often pay less than 1 per cent interest — which makes them one of the worst savings deals around.

If you usually keep your account in credit but occasionally stray into the red, look for a bank that offers the first £100 of overdraft free, or which has a buffer zone of £50 so that you do not pay interest and charges just because you miscalculated or overspent by a few pounds for a few days.

If you are nearly always in the red avoid interest-paying current accounts. The extra charges on these accounts for those who go overdrawn far outweigh any interest you may earn while in credit.

What you need to open a bank or building society account

A clampdown on money laundering means that an increasing amount of information is required in order to open a bank account. If you want to open a current account you will need to produce one or more of the following: a current passport, a driving licence, an armed forces card or a national insurance card — and in some cases a letter of reference from your employers.

For a current account your application should be processed within four days and you will then be given a cash card automatically. You may have to have an account up and running for three months to get a cheque guarantee card and six months to qualify for a three-in-one (cheque guarantee/cash/debit card).

Building societies require the same type of identification (or a credit card or bank cheque guarantee card) for a new cheque book account. It could take up to two weeks before the building society agrees to give you a cheque book account — they have to check your credit worthiness — and even then they could reject your application. However, because there is no risk to them, they can open a card cash account or high interest account for you within minutes.

Joint accounts

Warning

If you open a joint account with another person you are jointly liable for any debts even if you do not incur those debts yourself. Withdrawals can be made in two ways: with either signature or with both signatures. It depends on how much each partner trusts the other.

Banker's references

A reference may be required to get a loan or borrow from a third party other than your bank. If you request a banker's reference on someone else, bear in mind that they are notoriously vague and require you to read between the lines.

Guarantors

In order to get a loan, the bank may require you to find a third party to guarantee the loan. Alternatively, you may be asked to be a guarantor for a family member or friend. Check out the legal liabilities and also confirm the maximum amount you could be liable for. If you guarantee a loan and the repayments are not kept up, you could be liable for far more than the original amount borrowed once interest is added.

Banker's drafts

A banker's draft is a cheque which guarantees to pay the recipient the sum stated. They are used as a way for people to buy large items such as cars or expensive consumer goods without having to carry around large sums of money. The alternative is to pay for such items with a credit or charge card.

Banker's drafts are only given to customers of a bank and only those who can prove that they can cover the sum quoted on the banker's draft from their bank account. There is usually a charge of £10 or more for this service.

Warning

Once a banker's draft has been issued and handed over for goods it cannot be cancelled through the bank.

Building society drafts are not totally risk free. They have occasionally been stolen so the goods should never be handed over until your building society has confirmed that the draft has been honoured by the originator.

Direct debits and standing orders

Direct debits and standing orders exist to help you spread your bills over the year — usually in twelve equal sums (until there is an adjustment).

Direct debits

A direct debit is an automatic payment which transfers funds from your account to settle your bills as instructed. The company you are paying has full control over what sums are taken (if it wants to alter the amounts, then it should give you 14 days' notice). They are popular with mortgage lenders and service companies as they know they will be paid on time. However, the bank customer can cancel direct debits. (Write to both the bank and the company you are paying.)

If a direct debit is taken out of your account on the wrong day or is for the wrong amount and you suffer bank charges as a result, these should be reimbursed by the bank or building society as soon as you notify them.

Standing orders

Standing orders enable you to make a regular fixed payment from your account to another bank or building society account. This could be a good option for you if you have to pay regular bills for the same amount each month. Standing orders give you more control than direct debits, because you set them up and you can change the amount paid.

However, if the amount varies — such as with a mortgage repayment — direct debits can be a better method of payment as the amount is varied automatically (notice must be given to you in advance), saving you the effort of changing the amount yourself.

Understanding bank charges

Banking is usually only free if you are in credit. However, on some interest-paying accounts there are fees if you are not in credit above a certain amount and some building societies make no charges if you are overdrawn.

Bank charges and terms and conditions change, so keep abreast of any new charges or charge increases.

Every bank and building society must produce a tariff of bank charges every year. Make sure you keep this to hand so that you do not get a nasty shock when you ask for duplicate statements and are charged £20 for them.

Get to know the charging period. Most banks charge on a monthly basis. If you are overdrawn on the last day of the charging period and the first day of the next charging period, you will incur two lots of monthly fees.

Overdrafts

Remember that an overdraft is a facility — not a loan. As such it can be withdrawn or called in if the bank is not satisfied with the way you are handling your account or if it fears you will not be able to repay the debt. An overdraft should not be viewed as a permanent means of borrowing. Banks may charge an arrangement fee to set up a facility.

If you are constantly in the red you should go back to square one and look at your budgets again.

The cost of overdrafts — particularly those which are unauthorised — is very high. And remember, the major banks are getting tougher and cracking down on unauthorised overdrafts and charging ever higher penalties for going overdrawn.

It is better to have no savings at all than to have £1000 in a savings account earning 4 per cent net of tax and a £1000 overdraft being charged at 20 per cent.

£   **Money tips**   £

- Never borrow without agreeing the overdraft with your bank. Unauthorised overdraft interest rates are currently running at more than 30 per cent.
- Remember, overdrafts are charged on a daily basis and they can add up to more than you borrowed in the first place.
- There is often a fee for agreeing an overdraft limit.
- Get to know your bank's charges and terms and conditions. For instance, there is often a £50 buffer zone on overdrafts.

£   £

Personal loans

If you are borrowing for the short term, say for under six months, then an overdraft can work out to be a cheap way of borrowing money. But if you want to borrow for longer than that, consider a personal loan, especially for buying a car or an expensive consumer durable item. The payback period is usually one, two or five years (see Chapter 4 for more on loans).

£   **Money tips**   £

- Don't just ask what the monthly repayments will be. Always ask what the annual percentage rate will be. The APR is the true cost of borrowing.
- Loans tend to be given at a fixed interest rate which makes it easy to judge how much you can afford. If the rate is not fixed, you should be prepared for rates to rise to three times as much.

£   £

Secured loans

A secured loan allows a lender to protect the loan by obtaining a legal charge on an asset such as your home. The interest rates charged on secured loans are generally lower than on unsecured loans.

How to read your bank statement

Your bank account number consists of the sort code 00-00-00 and your personal account number. The statement also shows the sheet number and the date of the statement. Most importantly, it gives a rundown of all the transactions in the previous month: a column for withdrawals and another for deposits. And finally there is a total showing the balance.

Always check your bank statement.

How to use your cheque book

When you use your cheque book you will usually have to show your cheque guarantee card. This is usually required by the retailer to ensure that the cheque will be 'cleared' and they will get the sum shown. Guarantee cards usually honour cheques up to the value of £50, but you can ask your bank for a higher guaranteed amount such as £100.

Some supermarkets and shops accept cheques over £50 even if you only have a £50 guarantee. However, you may be required to provide identification such as a driving licence or passport and write your name and address on the back, although often they will accept the name and address of your bank.

If you are overdrawn on your account and you write out a cheque it could be rejected (bounced) and sent back to your bank branch marked 'refer to drawer'. Your bank will also write to tell you why the cheque has been returned — namely because of lack of funds. And you will usually be charged. You may be sent the cheque — particularly if it has been returned because you have failed to fill it in correctly.

A cheque that is covered by a £50 or £100 cheque guarantee card must be honoured if it is correctly filled in with the correct signature, whether or not you are overdrawn, because the card is a 'guarantee'.

If you lose a cheque or your cheque book is stolen, report it immediately.

If you want to stop a cheque being paid there is a charge. However, you cannot stop a cheque for less than £50 if it has been backed by a cheque guarantee card and has the guarantee card details on the back.

Combating cheque fraud

Cheque fraud is a constant worry. However, now the banks and building societies are issuing cheques with the words 'Account Payee' pre-printed in the crossing — the two vertical lines on the cheques.

This means that all bank and building society customers will have legal protection to ensure that the cheques they write are only paid into the accounts of the people for whom the money is intended.

A cheque crossed with the words 'account payee' cannot be signed on the back (endorsed) by the payee and paid into another person's account. It can only be paid into the payee's account.

This may not seem very different to the previous position, as people have been crossing their cheques 'account payee' for years. But the words had no legal status until the Cheques Act 1992 came into force on 16 June 1992. Now if a collecting bank allows a cheque which is crossed 'account payee' to be paid into the wrong account, it is liable for any loss.

The drawback is that those who do not have a bank or building society account — almost 1 in 10 of the population — will no longer be able to cash cheques through another person's account. However, it is still possible to pay a cheque in if you explain the situation to the manager and allow him or her to decide whether or not to accept it. In addition there could be problems if the name of the account holder is misspelt or if a married woman receives a cheque in her maiden name.

The new wording of the Act does not, unfortunately, prevent other types of cheque fraud. For instance, someone stealing a cheque sent through the post can get round the 'account payee' crossing by fraudulently opening an account in the payee's name, although this is increasingly difficult to do. In such cases of fraud, the innocent customer, not the bank, would have to meet the loss.

The Inland Revenue always encourages people to pay their tax bills over the counter at a bank, building society or the Post Office, rather than by sending cheques in the post. Equally, unless you have standing orders or direct debits for your utility bills (water, gas, electricity or telephone), it is best to pay them at the Post Office or the payment points in their own high street shops.

Money tips

To protect yourself, follow these tips:
● Write your cheques with a ballpoint or fountain pen, but not a felt-tip which is easy to alter.
● Leave no space to the left of the payee's name or the amount. This prevents words or figures being added. Fill in unused spaces with a thick line.
● Write your full signature against any alterations.
● Keep your cheque book and guarantee card safe, but not together.
● Write in capitals — they are more difficult to alter.

Clearing times

When you write a cheque out at a bank, or for goods and services, it usually takes three working days to clear, but it can take longer depending on when and where the cheque is paid in. Do not rely on this delay as clearing times vary from bank to bank. Ask the bank or building society what their clearance cycle is and when you will receive 'value' — that is, when you can draw against a deposited cheque and when you will start to earn interest on your deposit. Clearing times vary because the banks are in competition with each other. However, banks now issue a code of practice for personal accounts and these list clearing times.

Some building societies have ten day clearance (but will credit interest after three). This varies from society to society and also with the type of account you have, so check.

For debit cards, the clearing period may be only one day. Cash machine withdrawals are deducted at close of business. Again, clearing times can vary depending on whether you draw from your own bank's network of machines or another's, or whether it is an overseas transaction.

Cash dispensing machines

Most banks and building societies offer plastic cards to go with their current or savings accounts, which can be used in their cash dispensing machines — also known as cashpoints or automated telling machines (ATMs).

The major banks have crossover arrangements with other banks. For instance, the National Westminster has a crossover arrangement with the Midland, while Barclays has the same arrangement with Lloyds. Banks now offer a three-in-one card: debit card, cheque guarantee card and cash machine card.

Every bank issues a card separately from its associated PIN number. The PIN number is a four digit number which the bank asks you to memorise. Do not write down the number or give it to someone else, as you will not get a refund if someone uses your card fraudulently after you have divulged the number.

Some banks have cash machines that let you change the PIN number to one you can remember more easily.

The building societies also issue cards for cash dispensing machines. Many societies are members of a system called LINK, which allows you to draw cash from any member society's or bank branch's cash dispensing machines.

You usually have a limit of £100 or £200 that you can draw from cash dispensing machines in any seven-day period. If you go over that limit your card will be ejected. You can usually ask for this limit to be changed.

Complaining

If you have problems to do with your bank or building society you should complain. You should first speak to the bank manager at your local branch, and failing that complain to the customer care department at head office. If you still don't get any satisfaction, approach the Banking Ombudsman or Building Society Ombudsman (see Chapters 9 and 10 for procedures and addresses).

On the other hand, you could always switch to another bank or building society.

How to switch banks

If you change banks there can be problems with direct debits not being paid or standing orders going astray, and you could be stranded without a cheque book or cash machine card if you go about it the wrong way.

If you follow these tips everything should go smoothly:

1. Open the new account before closing the old one.
2. Set a transfer date for closing the old account about 5 to 6 weeks in the future to give yourself time to move all your direct debits and standing orders to the new account.
3. Inform your employer that you are changing banks, giving details of your new account so that your salary can be paid into the new account from the switch date.
4. Obtain a list of standing orders and direct debits from your existing bank.
5. Write to your existing bank and ask them to cancel all standing orders from the transfer date. Send a list of your standing orders to your new bank asking them to pay.
6. Write to everyone you pay by direct debit asking them for a new mandate form. Send the forms to your new bank and ask them to pay the direct debits from the transfer date. Contact your old bank and instruct them not to pay any more direct debits after the transfer date.
7. Switch over to your new account and leave enough money in the old one to cover outstanding payments. After that, you can close down the account.

Money tips

- Never borrow on an unauthorised overdraft — it can cost £120 just to borrow £60 for a month.
- Always check your bank statement and question bank charges if you think they are wrong.
- Never divulge your personal identification number (PIN) for your cash card to anyone. If someone else uses it with the correct PIN you will not receive any compensation for your missing cash.

3
Making your money work for you

You have to speculate if you want to accumulate. If you simply stash your cash in a savings account the chances are that you will not even beat inflation in the long run.

Of course, there are exceptions to this rule. When interest rates were in double figures, peaking at 15 per cent, and inflation was falling, it paid to be a saver. After all, the risks were low and the rewards — 10 per cent interest — were high.

Nevertheless, over the long term the risk/return ratio tends to work the other way round. The lower the risk, the lower the return. This is very true now when interest rates are at a historical low.

However, investors run the risk that they will not get all of their initial investment back — or any at all if they go for higher returns from high risk investments.

The risk of loss must be weighed against the risk savers run from the ravages of inflation. When inflation is low — as it is at present — it is easy to forget what it can do to your spending power in the long term.

It is still quite extraordinary how much you can save and how quickly the money mounts up.

For example, if you save £30 a month for five years and get an average interest rate of 5 per cent, you will have more than £2000 as a lump sum.

Similarly, if you save £60 a month for 10 years and manage to average 8 per cent interest a year, your money will grow to £11,000.

New Tab Friendly Society

● HAVE YOU EVER DISCARDED AN INVESTMENT SCHEME
BECAUSE YOU COULDN'T FACE THOSE ENDLESS FORMS?

You're Not The Only One

● HAVE YOU EVER ABANDONED THOUGHTS OF TAX-FREE
SCHEMES BECAUSE YOU THINK YOU CAN'T AFFORD THEM?

There Are Others Like You

They come to the New Tab Friendly Society - we've been helping people like them for over 100 years. Families, grandparents, students, all have benefited from our friendly, simple, secure savings schemes.

WHY DON'T YOU JOIN THE NEW TAB 'FAMILY' SOCIETY?

Write to: Mrs. Kathy Blomfield, Secretary, New Tab Friendly Society,
FREEPOST TK1837, TWICKENHAM TW1 3BR. Tel: 081 892 4969

Member of Lautro in relation to Life Assurance only

Established 1891

How to go about saving and investing

The first thing to decide is how much you want to invest, over what period of time and with what level of risk. Higher rate taxpayers should also look at the tax implications of any investment they make. There is no point in earning a 10 per cent yield if 4 per cent of this goes in tax and there is an 8 per cent yield on offer, tax free, from an alternative investment. Bank and building society savings are safe, but in the long run do not keep pace with inflation.

The types of investments available to everyone are described below. Make the most of the tax breaks.

Get more out of your savings. Get into unit trusts.

Shouldn't your hard-earned savings be working even harder?

The simple answer is unit trusts.

Experience shows that unit trusts have the potential to provide excellent returns. Better still, they're easy to understand and use.

Your money is in expert hands. It's easy to get your hands on your cash quickly, should you need to. And there can be attractive tax advantages too.

Whatever your savings needs, there's a unit trust for you. Don't you owe it to your savings to find out more?

For more details and a free information pack, call the Association of Unit Trust and Investment Funds (AUTIF) on 071-831 0898 or write to us at 65 Kingsway, London WC2B 6TD.

Making savings work harder

NATIONAL SAVINGS LUMP SUM INVESTMENT

National Savings offers unrivalled security and a variety of schemes for lump sum investments. The schemes are easy to purchase, and simple to operate. Where the interest rate is guaranteed it is fixed and unchangeable for the period advertised, unlike the so-called guarantees offered by some savings schemes where the guarantee is related to an often low, variable rate. National Savings also offers TAX-FREE savings products.

Probably the best known of National Savings lump sum products are Savings Certificates. There are two kinds, Fixed-interest and Index-linked. Fixed-interest Certificates offer a tax-free guaranteed interest rate. They must be held for five years to get the advertised return.

Index-linked Certificates are a safe hedge against inflation. They offer a tax-free guaranteed return on top of inflation proofing. They thus protect the purchasing power of your savings AND give a tax-free bonus as well. They must also be held for five years to get the advertised return.

For both types of Certificate the minimum purchase is £100 with a maximum holding of £10,000 per person (joint or sole) in each issue.

For all new purchases, before the end of five years, National Savings will inform holders that their Certificates are about to mature.

The newest product for lump sum investments from National Savings is the FIRST Option Bond, which caught the public's attention when they were launched in July 1992. Unlike any other National Savings product, tax is deducted from the interest at source, at the basic rate. This makes the bond particularly well suited for basic rate taxpayers.

The interest rate is guaranteed for 12 months at a time and National Savings will write to holders at each anniversary to tell them of the guaranteed rate for the next 12 months. The minimum purchase is £1,000 and there is a maximum holding (joint or sole) of £250,000. A bonus of 0.3% (0.4% gross) is payable for holdings of £20,000 plus.

Capital Bonds are a lump sum investment which are particularly attractive to non-taxpayers. Like Savings Certificates, the advertised interest rate is guaranteed provided the bonds are held for five years. However, unlike Savings Certificates, they are not tax-free. Interest is automatically paid gross and non-taxpayers do not have to fill in an Inland Revenue registration form. Interest is added to each bond on the anniversary of its purchase date and a statement of value is sent to the holder after the end of each tax year. It shows how much interest has been added to the bond. At the end of five years the bond is repaid in full with all the interest earned. The minimum purchase is £100 and there is a maximum holding of £250,000 in all series of Capital Bonds, excluding any holding of series A.

Savers who are looking for a regular income from their lump sum investment should consider National Savings Income Bonds. The interest is automatically paid gross. It is paid at a variable rate but National Savings give six weeks notice of every rate change. The interest is paid in the form of a monthly income on the fifth of each month and can be made directly to a bank or building society account. The capital remains unchanged. Any withdrawals require three months' notice. The minimum purchase is £2,000 and there is a maximum holding (sole or joint) of £250,000.

Further details and application forms are available from all post offices on all of these products. Alternatively call free on 0800 868700 for more information.

Fidelity PEPs.
Tax-Free
growth potential.
In 10 varieties.

No investor looking to find the most sensible home for a lump sum can afford to ignore the Fidelity range of PEPs.

Not only are all returns free of income and capital gains tax. But our low initial charge of just 2% means that **LOW INITIAL CHARGE** ▶ more of your investment is put to work.

There are 10 funds to invest in, each designed to suit different needs.

Fidelity is the world's largest independent investment management organisation, and commits extensive resources to on-the-ground research, before picking stocks for our funds.

For more information, talk to your Independent Financial Adviser, or call us free.

Fund name and launch date	Total Growth Performance	Average Annual Growth since launch
UK Growth (24.06.85)	+90.4% over 5 years	16.3% p.a.
Special Situations (17.12.79)	+74.5% over 5 years	24.7% p.a.
Recovery (7.11.87)	+39.9% over 5 years	9.6% p.a.
European (4.11.85)	+144.0% over 5 years	26.5% p.a.
European Opportunities (10.9.88)	+131.3% over 5 years	18.2% p.a.
International (9.7.90)	+45.5% since launch	12.0% p.a.
European Income (7.2.87)	+124.5% over 5 years	12.3% p.a.
Growth + Income (17.12.79)	+57.0%	19.1% p.a.
High Income Fund (8.2.93)	+20.5% over 9 months	n/a
Income Plus (10.11.80)	+43.6% over 5 years	19.0% p.a.

Source: Micropal to 1.11.93, offer to offer with net income reinvested

CALL FREE 9am - 9pm OPEN 7 DAYS.

0800 414191

Fidelity Investments™

PEPs held for less than three years are subject to a withdrawal charge of between 1% and 3% + VAT. Past performance is not guarantee of future returns. The value of a PEP and the income from it may go down as well as up and you may get back less than you invested. Tax assumptions may be subject to future statutory change and value of tax savings will depend on individual circumstances. Please note that it was not possible to invest in a PEP prior to 1987. Issued by Fidelity Nominees Limited, a member of IMRO.

FIDELITY

More and more people are finding that the stockmarket offers an attractive home for their money. And one of the most attractive forms of equity investment is a PEP – an investment allowed by the Government to deliver returns free of all tax.

This means that you pay absolutely no income tax on the money your savings earn. And you pay no capital gains on any growth your investment makes. These features make a PEP, over the medium to long term, an investment of great potential.

Because PEPs are so attractive, the Government impose a maximum limit on PEP investments of £6,000 per person in any tax year, plus £3,000 for a Single Company PEP. These limits apply to an individual, so a couple can make a total investment of up to £12,000 (£18,000 including Single Company PEPs).

With literally hundreds of plans available, the choice is bewildering. At Fidelity, we aim to provide one of the most comprehensive ranges available.

With 10 funds to choose from, you can look for maximum or income potential – or a combination of the two. This flexibility is also reflected in our wide range of contribution options; including starting with a lump sum of £1,000, saving regularly from just £50 a month or 'Phasing' your investment over 6 months.

Our initial charge of just 2%, right across the range, is among the lowest in the business, and means that more of your money goes to work for you from day one.

Of course, it's the performance of the PEP that is the most important consideration. As the world's largest independent investment organisation, our investment strategy relies on in-house resources: the research, analysis and finally the judgement of our 250 expert investment managers and analysts located around the world, rather than the received wisdom of others. Last year they made over 30,000 visits and contacts throughout Europe and the rest of the world, assessing individual companies 'on the ground' for business soundness and investment potential.

It's an approach that's worked well – over the last 12 months our funds have averaged growth of over 49%. Indeed, our Special Situations Trust and Recovery Trust are both in the top 10 of the 144 funds in the UK Growth sector.*

In short, when you invest in a Fidelity PEP, you can invest with confidence.

* Source Micropal, offer to offer with net income reinvested, 1.11.92–1.11.93.

Past performance is no guarantee of future returns. The value of a PEP and the income from it may go down as well as up and you may get back less than you invested. Tax assumptions may be subject to future statutory change and the value of tax savings will depend on individual circumstances. PEPs held for less than three years are subject to a withdrawal charge of between 1% and 3% plus VAT. Issued by Fidelity Nominees Limited, a member of IMRO.

The Skipton

Share Shop

BUY OR SELL YOUR SHARES WITH JUST ONE CALL

- 1% COMMISSION UP TO £5,000
- 0.1% ON EXCESS OVER £5,000
- MINIMUM COMMISSION £15
- £5 LIFE MEMBERSHIP

FOR DETAILS CALL

0532 444095

SKIPTON
BUILDING SOCIETY

Share
Shop

NATIONAL SAVINGS LUMP SUM INVESTMENT

National Savings offers unrivalled security and a variety of schemes for lump sum investments. The schemes are easy to purchase, and simple to operate. Where the interest rate is guaranteed it is fixed and unchangeable for the period advertised, unlike the so-called guarantees offered by some savings schemes where the guarantee is related to an often low, variable rate. National Savings also offers TAX-FREE savings products.

Probably the best known of National Savings lump sum products are Savings Certificates. There are two kinds, Fixed-interest and Index-linked. Fixed-interest Certificates offer a tax-free guaranteed interest rate. They must be held for five years to get the advertised return.

Index-linked Certificates are a safe hedge against inflation. They offer a tax-free guaranteed return on top of inflation proofing. They thus protect the purchasing power of your savings AND give a tax-free bonus as well. They must also be held for five years to get the advertised return.

For both types of Certificate the minimum purchase is £100 with a maximum holding of £10,000 per person (joint or sole) in each issue.

For all new purchases, before the end of five years, National Savings will inform holders that their Certificates are about to mature.

The newest product for lump sum investments from National Savings is the FIRST Option Bond, which caught the public's attention when they were launched in July 1992. Unlike any other National Savings product, tax is deducted from the interest at source, at the basic rate. This makes the bond particularly well suited for basic rate taxpayers.

The interest rate is guaranteed for 12 months at a time and National Savings will write to holders at each anniversary to tell them of the guaranteed rate for the next 12 months. The minimum purchase is £1,000 and there is a maximum holding (joint or sole) of £250,000. A bonus of 0.3% (0.4% gross) is payable for holdings of £20,000 plus.

Capital Bonds are a lump sum investment which are particularly attractive to non-taxpayers. Like Savings Certificates, the advertised interest rate is guaranteed provided the bonds are held for five years. However, unlike Savings Certificates, they are not tax-free. Interest is automatically paid gross and non-taxpayers do not have to fill in an Inland Revenue registration form. Interest is added to each bond on the anniversary of its purchase date and a statement of value is sent to the holder after the end of each tax year. It shows how much interest has been added to the bond. At the end of five years the bond is repaid in full with all the interest earned. The minimum purchase is £100 and there is a maximum holding of £250,000 in all series of Capital Bonds, excluding any holding of series A.

Savers who are looking for a regular income from their lump sum investment should consider National Savings Income Bonds. The interest is automatically paid gross. It is paid at a variable rate but National Savings give six weeks notice of every rate change. The interest is paid in the form of a monthly income on the fifth of each month and can be made directly to a bank or building society account. The capital remains unchanged. Any withdrawals require three months' notice. The minimum purchase is £2,000 and there is a maximum holding (sole or joint) of £250,000.

Further details and application forms are available from all post offices on all of these products. Alternatively call free on 0800 868700 for more information.

National Savings.
Security has never been
so interesting.

All too often these days, someone shouts "investment opportunity!", and fools rush in. Thus proving that it's not always a case of safety in numbers.

The smart money, however, heads for National Savings to discover an exciting array of investment opportunities, thoughtfully designed to suit individual needs.

And all with the lifebelt security you'd expect from National Savings.

So phone us free on 0800 868 700 between 9am and 4.30pm Monday to Friday.

If you're safety conscious, you won't find a better way to keep your head above water.

Tax-free investments

TESSA

What is a TESSA?

A TESSA is a Tax Exempt Special Savings Account. TESSAs are usually offered by a bank or building society.

TESSAs are very popular. Latest figures from the Inland Revenue show that more than three million people now hold a TESSA, and between them they have invested more than £10 billion.

There are two types of TESSA, fixed rate or variable. There are very few fixed-rate TESSAs but they can be a good bet if the rates fall after you have taken one out, as you will get a better rate of return, but if they rise then you will be the loser.

Who should invest in one?

Anyone aged 18 or over can open a TESSA, but you can only have one account at a time. However, a husband and wife can each have a TESSA.

How much can be invested?

You can put £3000 in a TESSA in the first year, followed by £1800 in each of the subsequent four years, up to a maximum allowable sum of £9000. You must keep all the capital you have invested in the account for the entire five-year term.

Where should I go to buy a TESSA?

There is no shortage of TESSAs to choose from and most banks and building societies offer one. Minimum investments generally vary from £1 to £100, with some demanding lump sums and others offering monthly savings schemes. In a few cases, tiered rates of interest are available and, at the top end, these can be at least 1 percentage point above the prevailing bank base rate.

Can I invest the whole amount in one go?

The rules for TESSAs prevent you investing more than £3000 in the first year, so some institutions have developed what they call feeder accounts linked to their TESSAs.

How does this work? When you open your TESSA, you invest £9000, with £6000 going into a feeder account. The initial £3000 is put into your TESSA, and on each anniversary of the TESSA, the permitted maximum is transferred from the feeder account into the TESSA. (Often the amount is less than £9000 as interest is accumulated over the four years.)

Feeder accounts infrequently offer a rate of interest that is superior to most non-TESSA accounts, but it is worth checking first.

What if I am not happy with the performance of my TESSA?

If you are not happy with the performance of your TESSA, and you are tempted by a better rate of interest elsewhere, you can move your account from one TESSA to another without losing the tax benefits. But you could lose out.

Some TESSAs offer bonuses to discourage you from switching to a different TESSA. A typical loyalty bonus would be 1 or 2 per cent of the money invested in the first year, payable at the end of the fifth year.

If you do decide to switch, the typical charge for transferring to another TESSA is £25. Instead of a flat rate, some institutions charge a certain amount of interest. But beware, in some cases these charges can easily wipe out any interest earned.

What about tax?

For basic-rate and higher-rate taxpayers, TESSAs should give a better return than other savings accounts. But if you don't pay tax, the tax advantages of a TESSA will be of no benefit to you. However, the gross return on many TESSAs might be better than you would get from many building society high interest savings accounts.

If a TESSA-holder dies before the five-year term is completed then the TESSA is closed, but no tax is payable on the interest.

Can I withdraw the interest or capital at any time?

If you withdraw any of the capital you lose all the tax benefits and your TESSA will be closed. You would then have to pay tax on the interest to date, regardless of how many years you have had your TESSA.

But provided your TESSA offers such a facility, savers can withdraw some of the interest early, but only as much as is left after a notional 25 per cent basic rate tax has been deducted from the total interest earned.

Where can I go for advice and further information?

Go to any building society or bank — or seek independent financial advice. But shop around.

Get the Inland Revenue's free explanatory leaflet, IR 114 *TESSA — Tax-Free Interest For Taxpayers.*

Money tips

- Remember, a husband and wife can each have a TESSA, so don't miss out.
- If you decide to open a feeder account, make sure the rates are competitive.
- Check what it would cost you to switch a TESSA — what the penalties would be and what the bonuses are for staying put.

PEPs

What is a PEP?

A PEP is a Personal Equity Plan. It is a means of buying shares, unit trusts or investment trusts without paying tax and can be used as a tax shelter. The income is tax free, along with the capital gain when you come to sell. There are some 870 PEPs and over 200 companies providing them.

Who should invest in one?

Anyone who is aged 18 and over, and who is eligible to pay UK income tax, can buy a PEP. This includes members of the armed forces serving overseas (but not their spouses).

How much can I invest?

You can invest £6000 in a General PEP and £3000 in a Single Company PEP, which invests in the shares of just one company. Husbands and wives have separate PEP allowances, allowing a total investment of £18,000 in any tax year. If you do not fully utilise your £9000 allowance before the end of the tax year your unused PEP allowance is lost forever.

You can only invest in a General PEP with one plan manager per tax year, you cannot split your £6000 allowance across PEP managers. However, you can use different PEP managers in separate tax years.

You can also invest regular sums of around £30 a month in PEP schemes.

Existing shares cannot be transferred into PEPs unless they are new share issues or company share schemes. However, shares can be swapped (for some unit trust PEPs), or exchanged for the majority of PEPs.

Where can I buy a PEP?

You can buy a PEP from a stockbroker, financial adviser, fund manager or bank or building society.

What can my PEP be invested in?

You can invest in British shares, ordinary shares of companies quoted on any EC stock market and 'qualifying' investment trusts and unit trusts. These are funds where at least 50 per cent of assets are invested

HOW TO AVOID
THE FRONT-END LOAD

What is the difference between a PEP promoted with a 6% front-end load and another with an initial charge of under 1%? The answer is usually nothing, other than the salesman's commission and excess profits for the unit trust group concerned.

Faced with the realities of recession, some unit trust groups decided to reduce their front-end charges by 3%, whilst continuing to pay brokers and salesmen a 3% initial sales commission.

We believe that brokers can, and should, also provide a service based on dramatically reduced costs. We have therefore reduced our initial commission from 3% to 1% on all unit trust PEP products.

Whether switching existing PEPs or purchasing new ones you may find that we can offer you better terms than any other broker in the market. Not only that! As a PEP specialist, our research material and regular client bulletins are more focused than those provided by other advisors.

If you would like details of our current recommendations and our publication "PEPs in Perspective" please contact us.

The value of shares and the income from them may fluctuate or fall. Past performance is not necessarily a guide to the future. The value of any tax relief conferred by PEPs is dependent on the investor's personal tax position. Levels, bases of, reliefs from taxation are all subject to legislative change.

THE PEP SHOP LTD

14 Gordon Road, West Bridgford, Nottingham NG2 5LN
Telephone (0602) 825105 Fax (0602) 455076

The PEP Shop Ltd is an appointed representative of Expatriate Advisory Services Plc, a member of FIMBRA in UK or other EC shares. A maximum of £1500 can be invested in 'non-qualifying' funds — overseas equity trusts.

PEPs that are made up entirely of £6000 worth of unit or investment trusts are becoming the most popular, because they provide investment in a wider ranging portfolio than share PEPs alone.

For some savers, especially those with time and knowledge available to manage their own PEP investments, a self-select plan is a better alternative. There are more than 80 available, offered mainly by stockbrokers.

A self-select PEP allows investors to choose the individual components of a PEP, although they must do this through an authorised plan manager.

Holdings can comprise stocks or shares in investment or unit trusts. The individual components can be traded whenever the plan-holder wishes, subject to dealing charges.

Flexibility is the key attraction of self-select PEPs, as there is freedom of movement. Someone with a corporate PEP who wants to switch money into another scheme has to go through the complicated procedure of effecting a transfer.

Investors considering a self-select PEP should consider the quality of the administration behind the scheme. This can only be properly assessed after a plan has been taken out. If it proves poor, investors should transfer their holdings to another self-select provider.

What can't my PEP be invested in?

You cannot invest in the shares of an unquoted company (all shares have to be quoted), or gilts, as they are excluded by the Inland Revenue. But some unit and investment trusts do offer funds where part of the portfolio is invested in gilts up to a 50 per cent ceiling.

How long do I have to invest for?

It is best to invest in unit trust and investment trust PEPs for at least five years.

Can I withdraw income or capital from my PEP?

A number of PEP managers now allow investors to take income on a monthly or quarterly basis. This income is tax free and does not need to be declared on your tax return.

You may also be allowed to take partial capital withdrawals from your PEP, although your PEP manager may levy a charge in the

You may also be allowed to take partial capital withdrawals from your PEP, although your PEP manager may levy a charge in the process.

What if I want to change my PEP plan?

If you are disenchanted with your PEP manager from a previous tax year, you can transfer your plan to another manager, although your current PEP manager may levy 'transfer charges'. Not all PEP managers accept transfers and others may charge an arrangement fee. Check before you go ahead.

However, if you want to transfer your PEP from one scheme to another — usually because of poor performance — such a transfer could cost 3 to 4 per cent of the PEP's value.

What are the charges?

Charges for unit trust PEPs are normally structured in the same way as plain unit trusts: an initial fee of about 5 per cent of the value of the investment and then an annual charge of about 1.5 per cent for the PEP provider's running costs, such as the collection of dividends and tax refunds. There are no extra charges. If you invest in shares or investment trusts there can be an extra fee.

Growing competition in the PEP market has led some managers to cut charges. But at the end of the day, finding the right fund manager to look after your money is more important.

Investors in self-select PEP schemes should ensure that they are not weighed down with charges. Fees levied by self-select managers can comprise an initial charge and dealing commission plus an annual management fee and dividend collection fee.

Where can I go for advice and further information?

Chase de Vere produces a PEP guide, which is the most comprehensive available. It includes information on more than 870 PEPs run by over 200 different managers.

Further details are available from:

Chase de Vere
63 Lincoln's Inn Fields
London WC2A 3JX
Tel: 071-404 5766

£

Money tips

- For those with smaller sums, as little as £30 a month can be invested.
- A husband and wife each have an allowance.
- All income and dividends are free of income tax.
- All profits generated in a PEP are free of capital gains tax.
- You can either have income (dividends) reinvested or can have it paid out gross (tax free).
- You are restricted to taking out a PEP with only one scheme manager each year. A total allowance for any year cannot be split between two or more management groups — but you can switch from one PEP manager to another. Single company PEPs can be managed by a different firm.
- You should look for performance first and compare costs. Remember it is far better to pay 2 per cent charges on a 7 per cent yield — giving 5 per cent net — than to pay 0.5 per cent on a 5 per cent yield.
- A PEP must be managed and administered by a Registered Scheme Manager approved by the Inland Revenue and authorised under the Financial Services Act.

Pensions

What are the advantages of pensions?

Pensions are one of the most tax-efficient ways to save, as the Inland Revenue puts in £25 for every £75 you invest — or more if you are a higher-rate taxpayer, as you can get tax relief at your top rate. (See Chapter 8 for more on pensions.)

SAYE — Save As You Earn

What is SAYE?

SAYE are schemes which give tax-free bonuses to those who make a regular savings contract with a bank or building society. The bonuses are added on the fifth and seventh anniversaries, and the monthly maximum investment is £20.

A separate SAYE contract may be taken out with a building society, bank or from National Savings if the account is linked to a share option scheme, with deductions made from your salary.

What are the advantages of a SAYE scheme?

SAYE schemes are an ideal way to buy shares with little or no risk and no tax liability.

No tax is paid on the difference between the cost of buying the shares and the market value when the share option is exercised, provided the cost of the shares is paid out of the proceeds of a linked SAYE scheme.

An increasing number of firms offer these share schemes as an extra perk and incentive for staff.

Employees can pay between £10 and £250 a month with the option to exercise the share option after five or seven years. Employees gain because the scheme grants an option to buy shares at today's price. If the price of the shares falls, the employees can simply keep the proceeds of the SAYE contract with any interest or bonuses received tax free.

National Savings

What are National Savings?

Along with taxes and gilts, National Savings are another set of schemes to raise money from the public. Since government borrowing soared and the Treasury needs to raise cash to fund it, improved rates have made National Savings very popular.

What tax-free National Savings products are there?

A number of five-year National Savings products are tax free with guaranteed rates of return. These include:

- The 7th Index-linked Savings Certificates guarantee (at the time of going to press) to pay 3 per cent above inflation when held for five years. The minimum investment is £100 and the maximum £5000. An additional £10,000 of mature Savings Certificates and mature Yearly Plan Certificates can be reinvested. However, there are penalties if you cash in before completing the five-year term.
- The 41st Issue is a fixed interest Savings Certificate which guarantees to pay 5.4 per cent per annum compound when held for five years. The maximum investment is £5000.
- For those without lump sums to invest the Yearly Plan may be a better option. It pays 5.4 per cent per annum compound, guaran-

teed if 12 monthly payments are made and the plan is held for a further four years. Each further year's payments buy another certificate. The minimum investment is £20 a month and the maximum £400. Again, there are penalties for cashing in the investment early.

- The first £70 of interest on the National Savings Ordinary Account is tax exempt (so a couple can earn £140). However, the interest is generally lower than other rates.

- One of the best rates paid by National Savings is on the Children's Bonus Bonds. However, holders must be under 16. They are ideal gifts to children, paying 7.35 per cent per annum compound guaranteed when held for five years. The minimum investment is £25 and the maximum holding is £1000 in all issues. Again, there are penalties for early repayment with no interest earned on bonds cashed in before the anniversary purchase.

Income Bonds, Capital Bonds and the Investment Account all pay gross interest where no tax is deducted, but taxpayers must declare this and pay tax on the interest.

Premium Bonds

Premium Bonds are a form of lottery as there are no guaranteed returns, and are the other major tax-free National Savings Scheme.

As this is a Government 'lottery' your capital is guaranteed and protected by the Government. About £2100 million is currently invested in Premium Bonds. You get no interest on your investment.

Premium Bonds are a gamble, but at least you don't lose your capital, and winning is tax free. You can invest anything from £100 to £10,000. Bonds have to be held for three clear months before being eligible for the draw.

Prizes range from £500 to a top prize of £1 million. There is a monthly draw of two £100,000, three £50,000 and four £25,000 prizes.

All application forms and leaflets for National Savings products are available from Post Offices or direct from:

National Savings Despatch Unit
Room 073
Charles House
375 Kensington High Street
London W14 8SD

Rates are current at the time of going to press.

Friendly societies

Before the arrival of the welfare state, friendly societies supported members by paying sickness and unemployment benefits and widow's pensions. They are similar to building societies in that they are owned by the members, but they sell life assurance-based plans, some of which are tax free.

What tax-free investments are there?

Investment is restricted to £200 a year for single investments, and £18 a month for regular savings.

Like most life assurance investments, you can cash in the policy before the term is up, but you may not receive back your original investment.

Where can I go for advice and further information?

The Registry of Friendly Societies
15 Great Marlborough Street
London W1V 2AX
Tel: 071-437 9992

Investments which are taxed or taxable

For long-term investments and to get your money working for you, you should look at the stock market for real returns.

But you should not even consider investing in more adventurous investments until you have a step on the housing ladder, looked after your pension and life assurance needs and built up savings in risk-free bank and building society accounts. Risk is inseparable from investment which offers the prospect of capital and income growth.

Unit trusts

What is a unit trust?

A unit trust is a pool of investors' money invested in shares on their behalf by a fund manager. Instead of buying shares in a company, investors buy a share, known as a unit, in a trust. The value of these units can fall as well as rise, but unlike a bank or building society you may not get your initial investment back.

Some £70 billion is invested in these funds. There are more than 1300 unit trusts available run by more than 150 companies.

What are the advantages of investing in a unit trust?

The size of the unit trust means that a wider range of shares and investments can be bought than would be possible for a modest investor. This spreads the risk and the costs. Unit trusts also make it easier for investors to put money into overseas shares.

How long do you have to invest for?

Investors can buy and sell unit trusts at any time, but should be prepared to tie up cash for around three to five years.

What are the charges?

There is an initial charge of around 5 to 6 per cent and an ongoing annual management fee of between 0.75 and 1.75 per cent. However, each company has different charges and there have been moves to cut the costs. There is also a bid/offer spread — between the buying and selling price. The difference between the two is around 5 per cent, although the maximum possible spread is 9.5 per cent.

What do they invest in?

Unit trusts mainly invest in shares but can also hold money in cash, gilts, property, futures and options.

Where can I buy a unit trust?

You can get investment recommendations from an investment adviser (ring the IFA Promotion on 0483 461461), or you can buy direct from a leading unit trust company.

Picking a unit trust

If you had invested £100 in the best performing unit trust five years ago it would now be worth £390. But if you had picked the worst, you would be left with just £30 of your original investment.

With a bewildering choice of unit trusts on offer it is difficult to know if your money is being looked after by a top performer or a laggard.

More than 40 per cent of all money invested in unit trusts is in just 70 of the 1300 or so trusts on offer. More than 400 trusts have less than £5 million each invested in them.

Past performance is no indication of future performance. There is no guarantee that a fund that is at the top of the league today will still be there next week.

What are the risks?

Not all unit trusts offer the same degree of risk. The more cautious can invest in bond funds — such as government and corporate fixed-interest securities.

Broadly, the more specialised the underlying investments, the more volatile will be the performance of the trust. An investment in a unit trust specialising in small companies is riskier than one in well-known, large, blue-chip companies, even if the potential rewards of the former are greater.

Unit trusts investing in narrow geographical markets are also more perilous than national stock markets. An investment in Malaysia may be adventurous, but it is generally more volatile than a mature market like Japan.

How do you make money?

Unit trusts pay an income, and you can make a capital gain. Most unit trusts pay out income on an annual or half-yearly basis, but an increasing number offer a monthly income facility.

The advantage of income from a unit trust is that the level of income should rise over the years, rather than remain static or fall, even if dividends are cut.

Several unit trusts are now paying returns of 8 per cent and more, with the aim of providing an income better than the building societies and banks. (But beware, your capital could be used to fund this income).

How much can I invest?

Generally a lump sum of £500 or £1000 can be invested, but this can be much lower. More than 60 unit trust companies run monthly savings schemes, and the minimum monthly subscriptions range from £20 to £50.

Unit trust savings schemes are flexible — contributions can be stopped at any time without incurring penalties — and they are an ideal first step into the stock market.

BWD Rensburg Unit Trust Managers Limited was formed in 1985 as the Yorkshire General Unit Trust Limited. Since the launch of its first trust the company has moved on to managing six trusts with over £15 million worth of assets.

The Company is part of the BWD Securities Group PLC, which can trace its origins back over 100 years and currently manages in excess of £1.4 billion of clients' money. The Group is one of the largest regional stockbrokers, having ten offices around the country.

The BWD Balanced Portfolio Trust invests principally in UK quoted companies, fixed interest stocks and British Government Securities. Whilst the equity exposure will predominatly be towards blue-chip companies, investments may be made in smaller companies.

The BWD Cash Deposits Trust invests in UK authorised bank and building society Money Market Accounts, aiming to achieve higher interest rates for investors than those available from Instant Access Accounts.

The BWD UK Equity Income Trust aims to provide capital growth and a yield greater than the FTA All Share Index. At least 85% of the Trust is invested in equities and/or convertible stock, all investments are UK based.

The BWD International Growth Trust invests in a diversified portfolio of international equities covering all economic and geographical sectors, with the aim of providing above average capital growth.

The BWD UK National Smaller Companies Trust invests in UK Smaller Companies. At least 80% of the Trust's assets are invested in UK companies which form part of the Hoare Govett UK Smaller Companies Index.

The BWD Yorkshire General Trust invests at least 50% of its assets in Yorkshire companies, with the aim of providing capital growth over the medium term.

What about tax?

Income tax is deducted on dividends at the basic rate. Higher taxpayers will have to pay extra and non-taxpayers can reclaim the tax paid.

Investors could also be liable for capital gains, which must be declared to the Inland Revenue, but only if their gains (not the amount they sell) exceed £5800 in one year. But by investing through a PEP, unit trusts can be tax free. This means that investors can place £6000 a year into unit trusts through a PEP, and secure a long-term tax-exempt investment for themselves.

Where can I go for advice and further information?

The Association of Unit Trusts and Investment Funds
65 Kingsway
London WC2B 6TD
Tel: 071-831 0898

£   **Money tips**   £

- Remember, although there is every chance that the initial investment will grow, it can also fall.
- Do not put all your capital in a unit trust.
- Do not invest in a unit trust if you think you might at some stage in the future need to withdraw the cash in a hurry.
- Pick a low-risk general investment trust from a well-known institution if you are a beginner and do not have too much money to lose.
- Watch out for capital gains tax.
- Try to hold as much of your unit trust investment as possible in a PEP.
- You can keep track of the performance of your unit trust shares by checking the unit price in the national newspapers.

Investment trusts

What is an investment trust?

An investment trust is a quoted company on the London Stock Exchange — just like any other quoted company such Tesco or Guinness — which has collective investments. Instead of buying a share in a trading company, you buy a share in an investment trust and its funds. This pool of investment funds is in turn invested in a range of shares in other companies, in start-up ventures and in property.

The investment fund collects dividends from these investments and passes them on to the trust's shareholders. The value of the shares rises and falls with the underlying value of the investments, as with unit trusts. However, investment trusts offer a good spread of risk across a varied portfolio of shares.

Figures from the Association of Investment Trust Companies (AITC) show that £100 invested in a general UK investment trust ten years ago would have been worth £480 by the beginning of August 1993, compared with £205 if it had been deposited in a building society account.

The industry has a total of more than £34 billion under management in around 265 trusts.

How much can be invested?

You can invest as little as £20 a month in the regular savings schemes run by most large investment trusts. There is usually no maximum investment limit.

Or you can invest from between £250 to £500 as a one-off lump-sum investment and spread your money round a far wider range of shares than if you were to buy them individually yourself. This reduces the risk and the costs. If you invest in a PEP it will then be tax free.

The advantage of investing little and often is called 'pound cost averaging'. This evens out what you pay for your shares.

So instead of investing £1000 for shares worth £1 and then seeing them fall to 50p before rising to £1.50, investors can buy some shares at £1 but get twice as many for 50p and benefit from a larger gain.

What kind of shares are there in investment trusts?

Investment trusts offer a wide choice of investment funds: some are general or international funds; others specialise in more risky geographical areas and emerging markets; others still concentrate on high income or capital growth; or on venture capital and development funds, and property companies, smaller companies and unquoted companes. The narrower the specialisation, the higher the risk.

There are different types of shares in investment trusts and these range in risk and return. Most investment trusts consist of ordinary shares, but split-capital trusts contain several different types of shares, usually income shares, capital shares and zero dividend preference shares, as well as warrants.

Where can I buy them?

Until a few years ago, you could only buy investment trust shares through a stockbroker or bank, as with other shares, but many investment trust groups now run savings schemes so that investors can buy shares through the company at reduced rates.

What are the risks?

Investment trusts have a fixed number of shares which can be bought and sold on the stock market, the price fluctuating according to demand.

Most investment trusts have the added risk that they can trade at a discount (ie that the investments are worth more than the investment trust shares), called net asset value (NAV), or at a premium (when shares are worth more than the underlying investment).

For example, if you pay 80p for a share and the NAV is 100p, you buy at a 20 per cent discount. For 80p you enjoy the benefits of investments worth 100p. And if you eventually sell for 90p, the discount will have narrowed; while if you sell for 70p, the discount will have widened.

What are the charges?

One of the greatest attractions of investment trusts is their competitive fee structure. Other savings and investment products, including endowments and insurance bonds, have higher charges and are less flexible.

Despite recent increases, the average annual charge on investment trusts is still well below 1 per cent. The average discount at present stands at just 8 per cent because of demand.

On average, stockbrokers now charge commissions of about 1.8 per cent for small to medium-sized deals. There are bid/offer spreads and dealing charges. The cost of buying and selling through a Savings and Investment Scheme can range from nil to 4 per cent.

To this has to be added stamp duty of 0.5 per cent on every purchase. However, in some instances the only charge made on a scheme is the statutory stamp duty.

Where can I go for advice and get further information?

The Association of Investment Trust Companies
Park House

6th Floor
16 Finsbury Circus
London EC2M 7JJ
Tel: 071-588 5347

£ ———————————————————————————— £
Money tips

- Investment trusts tend to pay income either annually, six monthly or on a quarterly basis. To get a monthly income, invest in a range of trusts which have different dates.
- Investment trust shares rise and fall like other shares.
- They can be tax free if investors have a PEP. Not all trusts qualify for a £6000 tax-free PEP and some give only £1500 of tax-free investment. So check first.

£ ———————————————————————————— £

Life assurance/investment bonds

Life insurance bonds are investment funds run by life insurance companies. They can be set-term investments — usually 10 years.

They can be either unit linked (similar to a unit trust in that the returns are linked to the performance of units in a fund), with profits (which iron out the rises and falls in the stock market by paying out annual bonuses based on investment returns during the year plus a final bonus at the end of the term) or unitised with profits (a simpler version of the with-profits contract). (See Chapter 5 for more on life assurance.)

Two of the most common life insurance bonds are described below.

Guaranteed income bonds

Guaranteed income bonds (GIBs) are fixed term bonds. The word 'guaranteed' simply means that the rate is fixed and the original investment is repayable in full at the end of the term.

Interest on GIBs is paid net after deduction of tax, which is not reclaimable even by non-taxpayers. For higher-rate taxpayers the tax structure can make GIBs particularly attractive.

Maximum investment plans

Maximum investment plans (MIPs) are high investment, endowment insurance savings policies that are invested in units or funds. They usually last for 10 years. The minimum premium is about £10 a month, and there is no maximum investment. The proceeds at maturity are tax free.

You get regular premiums and you can take advantage of the tax-free income on policies held for ten years.

Permanent interest-bearing shares

Permanent interest-bearing shares are shares in building societies issued by building societies and quoted and traded on the London Stock Exchange. Permanent interest-bearing shares (PIBS) guarantee a set rate of return and pay an above average fixed rate of interest. But the price of PIBS can, of course, go down as well as up.

The shares are irredeemable and the only way you can get your capital back is to sell them.

How much can I invest?

Minimum investments vary from £1000 to £50,000.

What are the returns?

Interest is paid six monthly net of basic rate tax, and no capital gains tax is payable on profits.

What are the risks?

PIBS are a relatively new type of share and although they offer a high fixed interest, unlike other building society investments your capital is at risk. PIBS are not covered by the building society savings compensation fund and therefore PIBS holders are the last in line in the unlikely event of a building society being wound up.

Shares

Companies raise money from the stock market by issuing shares.

Share prices can rise and fall for a number of reasons: the profits and future earnings expectations of the company, the demand for shares, the prospects for the economy as a whole and the movements of stock markets in the UK and abroad all affect the share prices.

Stockbrokers and the financial pages of newspapers give advice on which shares to buy and sell. A private client advisory service from a stockbroker can be expensive.

Look at the P/E (price/earnings) ratio which gives an indication of how popular a share is. Generally the higher the figure of the ratio, the better the share.

How do I invest?

Unless you have large sums of money and are prepared to take a gamble, shares are not always the best bet. The cost of stockbroker's commissions and the risks of investing in just one or two shares often outweigh the rewards.

However, there are execution only (dealing only) share services which are the cheapest, charging from around £15. There is also 0.5 per cent stamp duty to pay.

Spreading your risk by investing in a wide range of shares is ideal, but it is hard without a large pool of cash. And once the costs of dealing are taken into account shares become very expensive.

What are the risks?

Shares are among the riskiest investments because you can lose all your money if the company goes bust. However, they offer the greatest potential return. Here's an example:

● If you had invested £1000 in Polly Peck, Asil Nadir's company, in 1979, you would have become a millionaire by the end of the 1980s. But if you had hung on to them, you would have lost it all when the firm went bust.

Further information is available from:

The Securities and Futures Authority
12 Old Broad Street
London EC2N 1EQ
Tel: 071-378 9000

Local authority investments

Like central government, local authorities need to borrow short-term and long-term funds. But money lent to local government authorities is not guaranteed, and so the returns are usually higher than British Government stock to reflect the higher risk.

There are two main types of local authority investment, described below.

Local authority loans

Local authority loans are lump sum investments paying a fixed rate of interest for a fixed period of time — usually from one to ten years.

You can invest as little as £100 and there is no maximum, but you cannot withdraw your money until the end of the term. Your money is locked up and only death will usually release it.

Interest is normally paid every six months. Interest is paid net of tax, and higher-rate taxpayers pay extra.

Yearling bonds

Yearling bonds are issued for a fixed period of a year. There is usually a minimum investment of £1000.

Futures and options

These are among the highest risk financial products available, and although the returns can be spectacular so can the losses. Only those with a good understanding of the risks involved should look at trading options, and particularly futures, themselves. However, there are a number of funds which are available to investors which make significant use of futures and options contracts and which may be the best means of gaining exposure to these investment instruments.

Futures

Futures have been around since the Middle Ages, and are now available on a wide range of underlying assets, from copper to stock indices (like the FT-SE 100 Index). At the time when a futures contract is traded, the buyer and seller agree the price which will be paid for the underlying asset, which will be exchanged at a fixed time in the future. Only a small proportion of the agreed amount is paid at the time of the trade. Futures can be traded, so the buyer of a contract whose price rises, may sell that contract at a higher price, before the original contract has to be delivered, thereby making a profit.

While investors only part with a proportion of the investment, they make profits on the entire contract. This means that only a small move in the price can lead to a massive profit. So, for instance, if an investor parts with £1,000 on a £10,000 contract and the price increases by 10 per cent, they would make a £1,000 profit.

But likewise, if the price falls by 20 per cent the investor loses not only the £1,000 original investment but £1,000 on top. If the price falls even further losses can mount up to several times the original investment.

Options

Exchange-traded options, like futures, are available on a wide range of underlying assets. However, the most familiar options are those which are available on the shares of companies. A buyer of an option contract has the choice to buy, or sell, shares in the underlying company at a fixed price at any time up to the expiry date of the option.

At their most simple, options offer individual and institutional investors the opportunity to participate in share price rises, for a known and limited risk. Options can be used as an alternative to shares for a straightforward play on price movement and can be used either in conjunction with a holding in the underlying shares, or by themselves. In this way they can be used to hedge against share price falls. If an investor has a large shareholding in a share they can buy an option on the price falling. So, if the share rises they gain and if it falls they can exercise the option to recoup some of their losses.

LIFFE, The London International Financial Futures and Options Exchange, runs courses for private clients who wish to know more about equity and index options. Details of these can be obtained by contacting LIFFE at:

LIFFE
Cannon Bridge
London EC4R 3XX
Tel: 071-623 0444

Money Markets

Banks and financial institutions earn interest on their deposits by placing them on the money markets. They shop around to get the best rate and because they have such vast sums to invest they can get a higher rate than is on offer to normal investors.

Minimum investments are high, however investors with smaller sums now have access to these higher rates through unit trusts.

Offshore

Accounts in tax havens which are not liable to local tax are known as offshore investments.

Although Luxembourg is the primary offshore investment base, others include the Isle of Man, the Channel Islands, Liechtenstein and, further afield, Bermuda, the Bahamas and the Cayman Islands.

Interest is paid gross without deducting tax. However, these havens are now of less interest to UK residents (other than those who are domiciled overseas) as any interest earned must be declared.

One of the most important developments in recent years has been the introduction of the Undertaking for Collective Investment in Transferable Securities (UCITS). This requires compliance to set standards, but also allows UCITS registered funds to be marketed across EC borders.

Only the Isle of Man operates a Depositor Protection Scheme, while building societies offshore through subsidiary companies are obliged, under S.22 of the Building Societies Act 1986, to discharge the liabilities of wholly or majority owned susidiaries.

Missing millions

There are millions of pounds unclaimed in various savings accounts and investments: unclaimed dividends, premium bond prizes, and bank and building society accounts.

Social security benefits are not always claimed (some £800 million of welfare benefits) and therefore save the Government millions of pounds in handouts.

Why is so much unclaimed? People forget, they change their address, they don't know what they can claim in benefits, and share certificates can be overlooked when a shareholder dies.

How to make the most of your savings

This chapter has looked at the different investment and savings schemes on offer to the average investor. However, you should not forget the basic savings account. It is essential to set aside money for a rainy day in an easy-to-access savings account before you start to put money into more long-term or more speculative investments.

Watch out for poor rates of return and also for changes in rates. Remember, a building society or bank account which has a high rate of investment today may not be such a good deal in future. Building societies have a habit of launching special savings schemes with high rates of return which lock investors in for months or even a year. Rates are then cut but investors cannot switch out of the scheme without losing interest — some have penalty periods of 90 days' interest if you pull your money out early.

However, investors do get a higher rate of return the longer they are prepared to save for. One-year term and 90-day notice accounts tend to offer higher rates of return, as do those with large minimum investments. Also watch out for tiered rates. If your savings fall below a certain level the rate of interest can be cut dramatically.

Warning

Many savings accounts do not even beat inflation and once tax is deducted can pay less than 1 per cent interest. It is up to you to keep a regular check on the rate of interest your savings are earning and to shop around for the best deal. Only keep enough in your instant or easy-access savings account to pay for emergencies (up to three months mortgage payments). Anything over that amount should be put to a better use, either in an investment scheme or higher paying longer-term account.

National Savings.
Security has never been
so interesting.

All too often these days, someone shouts "investment opportunity!", and fools rush in. Thus proving that it's not always a case of safety in numbers.

The smart money, however, heads for National Savings to discover an exciting array of investment opportunities, thoughtfully designed to suit individual needs.

And all with the lifebelt security you'd expect from National Savings.

So phone us free on 0800 868 700 between 9am and 4.30pm Monday to Friday.

If you're safety conscious, you won't find a better way to keep your head above water.

4

How to make borrowing work for you

The difference between credit and debt

Credit is the ability to borrow money in the knowledge that you have the funds to pay it back at a later date.

Debt is the inability to repay money owed for goods or services provided.

Methods of borrowing

Credit cards

If you want to borrow only a small amount for a short time, it may be better to use a credit card than, for instance, an unauthorised overdraft. It costs less than £20 to borrow £1000 on a credit card for a month — less than some banks charge for a letter telling you of an unauthorised overdraft. Overdrafts and credit cards are charged on a daily basis.

A credit card enables card-holders to buy goods and services without making an immediate payment. They are very useful when you want to buy an expensive item immediately.

You are allowed a certain agreed limit of credit by the credit card company. You have to pay a minimum amount (usually 5 per cent of the amount outstanding) to service the credit each month — unless you pay the whole lot off within six weeks (or 56 days) when you are not charged any interest (some cards have shorter periods). You are only charged interest on whatever amount is still outstanding. There may be an annual fee to pay for the use of a credit card. This is usually around £10 to £15.

● Purchase protection is an insurance against theft or accidental damage to what you buy with your credit card, usually for 90 days. It is offered by some credit card issuers.

- If you buy faulty goods costing more than £100 you should be protected under the Consumer Credit Act, which makes the card issuer jointly liable with the retailer, so you should get a refund.
- You are usually liable for only the first £50 of losses if your card is lost or stolen. But always report theft immediately.

How to make the most of your credit card

- Remember, interest is charged on credit card borrowing if you do not pay the outstanding balance in full each month. Therefore if you have an outstanding balance left from the previous month's statement, you will pay interest on this month's borrowing and not get an interest-free period. (Only the Save & Prosper card still offers an interest-free period to those who have not repaid their outstanding balance in full.)
- Don't wait until the last date possible to pay your credit card bill. By paying off the debt early you will be charged less interest. (Interest is charged on the daily outstanding balance.)
- Don't borrow over the long term on credit cards — the APR (annual percentage rate) is comparatively high.
- The best days to spend are on or just after the statement date (printed at the top). If you spend on that day, the item will not appear until next month's statement, so you have 25 days from then in which to settle your bill.
- Leave enough time for your credit card payment to be processed. It takes up to five days for your payment to be credited to your account. If you miss the payment date, you will have to pay interest.
- If you cannot settle your bill in full, but later you find you can afford to pay off more between statements, do so. Interest is charged on the amount outstanding each day, so it will reduce the interest charged that month.
- If you use your card to take out cash, there may be a fee (often 1–2 per cent of the amount of cash withdrawn). Or interest can be charged from the day you make the withdrawal. Read the terms and conditions of your credit card account.

- Always check your statement carefully. Mistakes are sometimes made, such as a charge from someone else's account ending up on your statement. If that happens, ring your central credit card centre immediately and ask them to check and then remove the entry.
- If you always pay your credit card bill in full each month pick a card without an annual fee.
- If you do not usually pay off your bill in full, go for a card that has an annual fee but a lower rate of interest.
- If you tend to spend by plastic in only one or two shops and always pay off your bill in full each month, consider a store card. It could be more convenient and there are often special offers attached.
- Always check that your credit card slip has been filled in correctly.
- To check out the best credit card deals, compare the card's monthly interest rates — credit card APRs are not always comparable.
- Beware of continuous debiting authorities. They are the credit card equivalent of direct debits but carry less consumer protection, so it is up to you to contact the company direct to cancel them.

Charge card

A charge card is like a credit card, only there are no pre-set spending limits. You have to pay off the full balance every month, so there is no interest charged. You have to pay a joining and annual subscription fee for these cards.

As well as standard charge cards there are also gold and platinum charge cards which offer you an overdraft or loan facility. You can use the overdraft to pay the charge card bill.

Standard charge cards

With charge cards the balance has to be paid off in full within a certain period of receiving a statement.

The advantage of charge cards is that there is no pre-set spending limit. You do not have to worry about running out of credit on an expensive holiday or when you buy an expensive household item.

Some lenders insist on direct debits for settlement. Most levy penalties for late payment, but there is also the risk that the card will be withdrawn if this happens too often.

The main disadvantage of charge cards is that they carry a higher annual fee than credit cards, usually about £80 a year.

But the annual fee is meant to be a charge for a whole range of perks. For many people, the most important of these is the chance to borrow money at preferential rates and without the usual arrangement fee and other charges.

Gold and platinum cards

To qualify for a gold card, which is basically a super charge card, you must have an income of at least £20,000 (but that can vary) to ensure that issuers know you have the means to settle your bills.

Some cards give overdraft limits of up to £10,000, but lending has been tightened up, so check first.

The perks on gold cards are numerous and include travel accident insurance, emergency cash and card replacement, legal and medical helplines, compensation for luggage delays or losses, and a refund of money spent on holiday when a travel company fails.

Another good perk which is offered by most gold card issuers is purchase protection for goods bought with the card (they cover damaged or stolen goods) — usually for 90 days.

You can also make cash withdrawals abroad and obtain cash advances from member banks at home. However, most banks charge a 1.5 per cent handling fee on such advances.

Platinum cards are similar to gold cards, but offer greater benefits and overdrafts. You just have to be wealthier to qualify for one.

Some issuers have an emergency replacement service for lost or stolen cards. But charge cards are not usually covered by the Consumer Credit Act, which limits the cardholder's liability to £50.

Store cards

Store cards are credit cards issued by retail chains. They are offered as a method of gaining customer loyalty. You have to beware, as these cards often charge the highest APRs of all the cards available. But if you settle your bill in full, you can claim customer discounts and get free credit.

Loans

Personal loans

A personal loan is a method of borrowing money from a bank or building society that spreads the payback period over a certain length of time — one, two or five years.

The interest rate is a flat rate over the time agreed. An overdraft may be a cheaper method of borrowing in the short term, say under six months. Watch out for arrangement fees.

Secured loans

Secured loans are normally cheaper than unsecured ones. Some borrowers have been duped into taking these on because 'secured' sounds like a safe thing.

However, it is safer for the lender not the borrower. It gives security to the lender, not you. It means that the debt is secured on an asset — usually your home — and if you fail to keep up repayments you are at risk of losing your home. The lender can apply to a court to repossess your home and then sell it to repay the debt. You might get a lower rate of interest with a secured loan but you do place a lot on the line. Make sure you can afford it.

The most common secured loan is a mortgage on a property. And the reason why mortgages are one of the cheapest ways to borrow is that they are secured on the property and the mortgage lender has the first call on your home if it is sold to repay debts.

£ **Money tips** £

- Loan rates tend to be lower if the amount is secured — eg on your home which is at risk if you fail to keep up with repayments.
- You can often get a cheap loan if you take it out when your buying certain goods. For instance dealers may give 0 per cent finance on particular cars, and some furniture shops make similar offers.

Credit unions

Credit unions are non-profit-making financial institutions that are owned by and operated for their members. Members of each credit union share a common bond — a local community, professional association, church or employers.

Credit unions exist to encourage regular saving, but are also there to make loans at attractive rates. They lend at an APR of just over 12 per cent at the time of writing, which is a good deal lower than many other forms of loan. You usually have to save for a while before you will be allowed a loan and the maximum is usually £2000 more than your savings.

You have to be a member of a credit union to benefit from these cheap loans. You can start your own credit union. (See also Chapter 3 on savings.)

Hire purchase

Hire purchase (HP) is instant credit offered so that you can make an instant purchase, particularly for electrical goods, but also for car purchases.

Hire purchase may be easier to get than other loans as the lender has your 'purchase' as security. But the monthly interest rates and APR can be very high. Beware of the APR on HP agreements — a bank loan might be cheaper.

To pull out of an HP deal after the cancellation period has ended, you must pay or have paid at least half the total cost and you must return the goods. If they are damaged, you will probably have to pay for repairs. You cannot sell HP goods until the agreement has been paid off.

Second mortgages

A second mortgage is a form of secured loan. However, it does not qualify for mortgage interest tax relief which is only given for a loan to purchase your principal private residence.

Mail order

Mail order is a handy way to shop as it is based on catalogues that you receive in the post. It is also a form of borrowing (credit) if you pay regular instalments over a number of months, instead of paying a lump sum. You won't have to pay any interest.

Pawnbrokers

You can get a loan from a pawnshop in exchange for leaving, for example, an electronic item or piece of jewellery. You get the item back when you repay the loan in the agreed time.

A pawnbroker charges high interest, up to 50 per cent APR, and if you don't pay the money back within a given period of time (usually six months) the item can be sold. Using a pawnbroker can be a very expensive way of borrowing.

Credit licences

Brokers who arrange finance have to be registered with the Office of Fair Trading and obtain a credit licence. However, this does not always guarantee that they will be reputable and if they walk off with your arrangement fee the chances of you getting it back are usually slim.

Loan sharks

The Consumer Credit Act 1974 contains provisions to deal with 'extortionate credit'. These are designed to protect consumers against loan sharks.

However, very few cases have been taken to court under these provisions and in only a handful of cases has the consumer won. The concept of extortionate credit is to be replaced with unjust credit so that the courts will in future take into account the way the loan was sold as well as the rate of interest.

Warning

Watch out for dubious loan arrangers. They often charge huge up-front arrangement fees. These can be as high as £1000 to arrange a £5000 loan.

Also watch out for the APRs charged. They can often be well over 100 per cent, and not only from loan sharks. The definition of extortionate credit is very vague. If proved to be extortionate the Office of Fair Trading can intervene, and a court can force the lender to cut the rate of interest. However, short-term, non-secured loans to high-risk borrowers can be charged at over 100 per cent APR without breaking the law.

Many credit offers are aimed at those already in debt. But borrowing your way out of debt is rarely a solution. It is far better to negotiate a reduced repayment with your existing, reputable lender than to fall for an even more expensive deal from an unscrupulous loan shark. And remember, as the loan may be secured on your property, if you fail to pay up you could lose your home. A bank or building society, on the other hand, is likely to be much more sympathetic if you get into arrears and they often employ debt counsellors to help you sort out your finances.

Credit scoring

You could be refused credit because you do not match the profile required by the lender. This can be very annoying if you have no debts and have never had any financial problems.

Lenders keep details of how they 'score' people very secret, for obvious reasons. They get their information from credit reference agencies. But generally if you are not on the electoral roll, are not a home owner, have not lived at the same address for a considerable length of time, do not have a telephone, have not been in the same job for long and have no other credit, it will be harder to borrow than if you meet these criteria. You get points for the information given on the application form. However, different lenders look at different criteria; although one lender may have turned you down, another may agree to credit. Lenders do not have to say why they have turned you down.

It may seem strange that if you have no debts at all you are deemed a worse risk than someone who never borrows. However, this is because credit reference agencies are used by nearly all lenders. They can see from your credit reference how you have managed credit in the past. If you have had a loan and repaid it on time every month, the lender knows that you can handle credit.

What are credit references?

You may also be refused a loan because of a poor credit reference. This could be because you have a County Court Judgement against you, or because you are in arrears on a debt.

What are my rights on credit references?

If you are trying to get credit for £15,000 or less you have a legal right to know the name and address of any credit reference agency that was approached for details about you.

To find out, you need to write to the shop or loan company that refused you credit and ask. You must write within 28 days of the last time you contacted them about the credit deal, and they must tell you the name and address within seven working days.

When you contact the credit agency you must send £1 (non-returnable), give your full name and address (with post code) and give any addresses you have lived at during the past six years.

The agency might ask for more details. It has seven working days from the day it receives your letter to send you your file or tell you it has nothing on you.

If you feel the facts on your file are incorrect you can ask the agency to change them. You first have to write to the agency asking them to remove or amend the entry which you think is wrong. Within 28 days the agency should confirm that it will remove or alter the entry or take no action. If the agency has replied in that time, you can send a 'notice of correction' to add to the file they hold on you.

If the agency amends your file or adds the 'notice' of correction, it must send the details to anybody who asked about you in the previous six months.

If the agency does not want to add the amendments it must get the permission of the Director General of Fair Trading, and you should be informed of this. The agency can refuse your notice if it thinks it is incorrect, frivolous, defamatory or scandalous.

If the agency doesn't reply to the letter enclosing your notice of correction within 28 days you can ask the Director General of Fair Trading to intervene in the dispute. After further investigations the Director General will decide how the matter will be resolved.

The Director General of Fair Trading
The Office of Fair Trading
Field House
15–25 Bream's Buildings
London EC4N 5BH
Tel: 071-242 2858

Credit reference agencies don't keep blacklists. Nor do they give opinions on whether you should or should not have credit, they simply give out information to lenders. It is up to the retailer or loan company to decide whether you are a bad risk.

Credit reference agencies do keep information about good payers as well as bad. They usually keep details concerning the following:

- *The electoral or voters' roll* If your address is on the roll this shows that you live at the address given on your application form.
- *County Court Judgements (CCJs) and bankruptcies* Records are kept of all the people taken to court for non-payment of debts. Even when a debt has been paid, agencies keep a CCJ on file for about six years. In the Scottish Sheriff's Court these judgements are called decrees.
- *Previous credit accounts* If you have had credit previously, an agency may have details of your record of payments. If you paid on time this is likely to help you to obtain further credit.

The four main credit reference agencies are:

CCN Systems Limited
Consumer Affairs Department
PO Box 40
Nottingham NG7 2SS
Tel: 0602 868172

Equifax Europe Limited
Consumer Affairs Department
Spectrum House
1A North Avenue
Clydebank
Glasgow G81 2DR
Tel: 041-951 1100

Credit Data and Marketing Services
CCA Department
Dove Mill
Dean Church Lane
Bolton
Lancashire BL3 4ET

Infolink Limited
Consumer Affairs Department
38 Whitworth Street
Manchester M60 1QH
Tel: 061-236 8511

Annual percentage rate (APR)

The APR is not the same as the interest rate — it includes most of the charges you have to pay on a loan. It shows the true annual cost of credit as a percentage. The higher the percentage, the more expensive the loan.

Debt — what if it all goes wrong

If you go into debt and cannot pay back what you owe on your over-draft, credit or charge cards, loans and so on, don't delay. Try to get help from a Consumer Advice Bureau.

Also contact your local trading standards officer or Citizens Advice Bureau if you have any problems with your credit references and scoring or the financial companies you deal with.

You can contact the Citizens Advice Bureau National Debtline on 021-359 8501.

5

Everything you need to know about insurance and assurance

Protecting your assets

Car insurance

Motorists must have at least third party cover by law. However, one in twenty drivers breaks the law by having no insurance at all and this represents about 1.25 million drivers in Britain. But it is essential to have cover — a car is stolen every minute and one in four drivers claims from an insurance company every year.

On the plus side, of the 15 million privately owned cars on the road, 10.5 million are covered by comprehensive insurance policies.

The level of cover you need is dictated by the age and model of your car and what you can afford.

However, there are different levels of protection.

- *Basic third party* cover is the cheapest and the legal minimum.
- *Third party, fire and theft* is the second cheapest, although the cover is limited. If you dent your car you cannot claim and if someone else damages your car and then drives off you could be left with a write-off but no compensation.
- *Fully comprehensive*, as the name suggests, covers most types of damage to your car and third party claims. And that is why the majority of private motorists on the road pick comprehensive cover. However, there are still exclusions — so read your policy wording carefully. For instance, you may be required to park your car in the garage overnight and may be refused a claim if your car is broken into when left in the street.

How to shop around for the best deal

Car insurance is one of the easiest types of insurance to shop around for. And it is worth the effort, as you could save yourself hundreds of pounds. You can either contact an insurance broker or insurance agent or go direct to an insurance company.

As car insurance is very much a commodity, telephone insurance companies, known as direct sellers, have sprung up in recent years. As they 'cut out the middleman' they can often (but not always) get you cheaper car insurance.

You can cut costs by restricting the number of drivers on the policy or by opting for a larger policy excess (on comprehensive policies only), which means you pay the first £50, £100 or £150 or even more of any claim for damage to the car. Third party claims are still paid in full.

Generally the older you are, the cheaper your insurance — until you reach the mid 70s. Some direct insurers will not cover those who have been driving for less than five years.

Equally, the fewer miles you drive, the lower the risk of an accident. As a result some insurers give discounts to those who only drive a few thousand miles a year.

For Financial Independence - Depend on Zurich Life

"It's just as well that we don't know what's ahead of us" - a commonly held, and probably true, belief.

Unfortunately life holds some very nasty surprises. Sickness, disability and death can devastate a family - and although no-one can be given immunity, the economic effects of the unexpected can be offset by careful planning. It isn't worth leaving the financial well-being of yourself and your dependants to chance, so, together with your Independent Financial Adviser, consider the Zurich Life 'Protection Triangle' which could provide the basic financial protection you and your family need.

▲ Income Security - Safeguards against the financial effects of long-term sickness or disability. Also known as 'permanent health insurance' it can provide an income right up to your normal retirement age, should you become unable to work. The plan is sufficiently flexible to allow for career breaks for women and includes other special features.

▲ Life Assurance Protection - 'Term' assurance is the simplest way of providing your family with financial protection in the event of death. For a modest outlay, arranged to suit your budget and needs, you can achieve a high level of protection which can be updated to reflect changing circumstances.

▲ Lifestyle Protection - The effects of contracting a defined 'critical illness' can be offset financially by a Zurich Life policy. Lifestyle Protection provides a lump sum, payable following 15 days' survival after diagnosis, which can be used for whatever purpose is required - for example adapting the home, paying off the mortgage or simply further investment.

AWARDS - PRODUCT AND SERVICE

"Best Term Insurance Product"
1991, 1992 & 1993;
Money Week / Sherwood.

"Best Life (Protection) Provider" 1992 & 1993;
Money Marketing / Express Newspapers.

"Award for Service Excellence" 1993;
Money Week / Sherwood.

* MONEY WEEK and MONEY MARKETING are recognised as leading weeklies circulating amongst Financial Advisers and providers.

Ask your Independent Financial Adviser to explain the special features of Zurich Life's protection policies and how they can be tailored to best meet your needs.

Alternatively, telephone or write for further details to our Head Office the address of which is below.

ZURICH
LIFE

ZURICH LIFE ASSURANCE COMPANY LIMITED

A member of LAUTRO for Life, Pensions and Investment Business.
A member of the Association of British Insurers and the Insurance Ombudsman Bureau.
Head Office: Hippodrome House, 11 Guildhall Walk, Portsmouth, Hampshire PO1 2RL. Telephone (0705) 822200.
Registered in England No. 676139. Registered Office: Zurich House, Stanhope Road, Portsmouth, Hampshire PO1 1DU.

Different models and types of cars present different risks. Cars are rated in bands, according to the value, repair cost and performance.

Where you live also has a major impact on costs as does the use of the car — whether it is for business or social or for domestic and pleasure.

'Hot hatches' come high in the rating bands because they are more likely to be stolen and they tend to be driven by younger, more reckless drivers, so there is more risk of an accident.

The age of your car will also affect your premiums as, usually, the older the car, the cheaper it is to insure as statistically older cars are involved in fewer accidents. However, if parts are hard to find or your car becomes a collectors' item, it could mean higher premiums.

Your occupation plays an important part in determining your premium. Civil servants and bank employees often find it slightly cheaper to insure their cars; whereas professional sportsmen, publicans and jockeys are among the professions that can find it more expensive.

A full no-claims bonus (usually a 60 per cent reduction on the standard premium) makes one of the biggest possible differences to your car insurance premiums. You have to build up five claim-free years to get the maximum no-claims bonus. If you make a claim you lose part of this bonus and must then gradually build up further bonuses in stages until you reach the maximum once again. You can often insure against the loss of your no-claims bonus with a separate insurance policy by paying an additional premium.

Even if you do have an accident or have made a claim, all is not lost. Insurers have different methods of dealing with proposers who have had an accident. Their treatment usually depends on the severity of an accident and the driver's age.

Are you properly covered?

Before making a claim, check your insurance policy. You could find that you are covered for more or less than you thought.

Some policies cover you for an overnight stay if you cannot continue your journey because of an accident. On the other hand, if you fail to take reasonable precautions to prevent theft (and this can be proved), then you may not be covered if your car is stolen. Insurance policies have rules about who drives the car, even if you have cover for any driver. So you might not be covered if you let someone without a licence or who has a bad record drive your car.

Will I lose my no-claims discount (NCD) if I have an accident?

The insurer of the driver who is to blame will pay any uninsured losses from the innocent driver.

The guilty driver will then lose his or her no-claims discount; the innocent driver will keep it.

The onus, however, is on the 'innocent' driver to pursue his claim against the 'guilty' driver or his insurance company.

What is 'knock-for-knock'?

Most companies have 'knock-for-knock' agreements. The insurance companies pay their own claim if their policy is comprehensive. It saves time. If one of the drivers is clearly not to blame, he or she will be able to keep the NCD, despite the knock-for-knock agreement.

If you think that another driver is to blame, but your insurance company disagrees, you can sue the other driver for your uninsured losses. If your action is successful, then the other driver's insurer should pay your claim and uninsured losses, and your own insurance company will then reinstate your NCD.

What if you are hit by an uninsured driver?

If you are the innocent victim of a crash caused by an uninsured driver, you may be able to claim from the Motor Insurers Bureau (MIB). You will have to pay the first £175 of all property damage, but you will keep your NCD. The fund will pay:

- claims for personal injury caused by uninsured drivers, whether or not the driver can be traced;
- claims for damage to property where the guilty party is known, but uninsured.

Should you always claim?

Sometimes the cost of losing your NCD is more than the cost of paying for the repairs yourself. If so, don't claim. That way you won't lose your NCD.

If an accident is your fault, or it can't be proved that it wasn't your fault, you may have to calculate whether or not it is worth claiming. Work out the cost of the repairs to your car and deduct any excess, then add the cost of the repairs to the third party's car and their uninsured losses — if you were to blame.

You then need to work out how much losing your NCD would cost you, to see whether the equation works out in favour of claiming or against. Don't forget to add on the costs for future years: it takes four years to build up your NCD and the costs over that time can add up to £2000 or more in extra premiums. However, most insurance policy wordings require you to disclose all accidents even if you do not claim — so you should notify your insurance company.

£ -- £

Money tips

- Watch out for policy excesses and exclusions.
- Remember, a cheap policy may prove to be expensive if your car stereo, children's car seats and other accessories are not fully covered.
- Even fully comprehensive policies are not as comprehensive as you may think. Always read the small print.
- Don't claim on your policy for minor damage as repairs may be cheaper than the extra insurance premiums.

£ -- £

Household insurance

Household insurance is the umbrella term that covers both home contents and buildings insurance. You can buy them separately or combine them into one policy. However, buying a package of a mortgage and several different types of insurance makes it difficult to compare costs, and you may end up buying insurance that doesn't meet your needs.

Home contents insurance

Fewer than 75 per cent of households have home contents insurance. But no one should be without home contents insurance. With a burglary every 24 seconds, it isn't worth running the risk. Even those in rented accommodation should consider cover. After all, if their landlord's furniture was stolen they could face a hefty bill.

The hardest thing to work out is how much cover you should get. Anything that is not part of the building itself and you would take with you if you move house counts as contents. This includes carpets, curtains and clothes as well as furniture and electrical goods. You need to add up the total value of all these items.

Some policies have a set level of cover based on your number of bedrooms and type of house (bungalow, semi-detached etc). This takes the guesswork out of deciding how much cover to buy.

There are two types of policy: new-for-old and replacement value only:

- *New-for-old* If you opt for new-for-old (most policies provide this type of cover), you should insure yourself for the replacement value of all your belongings. It is easy to work out the value of new items such as hi-fis and TVs, you just need to refer to your receipts. Older items, antique furniture and the like are more difficult. Look around furniture shops to find out how much your belongings would cost to buy again — or tune into the *Antiques Roadshow!*

- *Replacement value only* A few policies cover replacement value only. These are cheap policies for those who want limited cover. They only pay out enough to cover the second-hand value of goods that are damaged or stolen so any wear and tear is taken into account.

- There are also more comprehensive policies — which cover accidental damage, bicycles and possessions even when they are not in the home.

£ _____ £

Money tips

- Make sure you have enough cover, or else your claim may not be paid in full — or only the second-hand value of the goods may be given.
- Small print: always read the small print. You may be required to have five-lever mortice locks on the doors, window locks and even an alarm to validate your policy.

£ _____ £

Buildings insurance

Around 61 per cent of all households have buildings insurance cover. But there is no doubt that buildings insurance is a must for all those who own a home. Flat owners (leaseholders) should also check that the freeholder has taken out insurance.

The 'rebuild' value — how much it will cost to demolish and rebuild your home if it is destroyed by fire or suffers from severe irreparable subsidence — is the amount of cover you need.

This is often different from the sale value. A surveyor should be able to give an accurate figure. Alternatively, you could consult the Association of British Insurers' guide (see Chapter 10 for the address and telephone number of the ABI).

Your buildings insurance usually comes with an excess which means you must pay for the first £1000 of any subsidence claim. Buildings insurance also covers fitted kitchens and bathrooms.

Your mortgage lender may suggest (or insist) that you take out buildings insurance when you take out your home loan. However, you can shop around and cut the costs. But expect to pay a £25 administration fee to your mortgage lender for the privilege of getting a cheaper deal elsewhere.

£ --- £

Money tips

- Different insurers charge different rates for each postcode (a few still charge a flat rate but high levels of subsidence claims mean that more are setting their rates according to risk). However, as they have different claims experiences, some insurers may quote higher rates than those which have suffered few claims in your area. So it may pay to shop around.
- Be careful if you switch insurers part of the way through your time in a house, as if you make a subsidence claim the insurers may say that it happened before they took on the cover of your property.
- Remember, you could be overpaying or underpaying on your buildings insurance. So make sure you get it right. If it is too high you could be wasting money; if it is too low your insurance may not cover the cost of rebuilding.

£ --- £

Protecting your family

Life assurance

Life assurance is as essential as insurance to protect your home and car. Yet few people are adequately covered.

Those who should take out sufficient life assurance are those with dependants and those taking out a mortgage. And anyone running a small firm should also insure their life under a key-man insurance policy.

The experts believe that those with families need cover for up to

five times their annual salary. You should at least buy enough life insurance to cover your mortgage and to provide for your family.

You may have life insurance already under your company pension scheme, which should pay out a lump sum of between three and four times your annual salary.

There are many different types of cover. Some include an investment element. Below are the main types.

Term assurance

Term assurance can be a flat amount on a decreasing level of cover. It is usually the cheapest and most basic form of life insurance. The premiums depend on age and sex — the younger you are the cheaper it is. But if you go with this type, if you survive to the end of the policy you get nothing back.

Whole of life

Whole of life assurance is more expensive and protects you until the day you die. You pay premiums all your life and on your death a lump sum is paid out. The younger you are when you start the policy, the cheaper it is.

Endowments

Endowment policies are really investments usually used to back a mortgage, but they also provide life cover. As with term assurance, if you die during the policy term your estate will receive the sum assured (the amount of life cover). However, as they have a fixed term, when this ends you receive a tax-free lump sum. Policies are for a minimum of 10 years (although they can be cashed in earlier with a much reduced return).

There are several types of endowment:

- *With-profits* This policy guarantees you a lump sum at the end of the policy term. But this is only a minimum amount. Investors should expect to get much more from bonuses added to the policy.

  Most people in the UK hold a with-profits type of policy as they have been on offer for longer than other types of endowment policy.

  When you invest in a with-profits fund, some of your money goes into bonds and property, but most goes into the stock market, as in a unit-linked fund.

  The core of the with-profits system is two forms of bonus:

  - **Reversionary bonuses** These are added annually, cannot be taken away if a policy is held to maturity, and are expressed as a percentage of an underlying 'sum assured'. If you have a with-profits endowment policy and die during its term, your relatives will receive the sum assured plus all the accumulated reversionary bonuses.

  - **Terminal bonuses** However, your estate will not receive terminal bonuses on your death, because these are only added to the policy when it matures. They are meant to reflect performance over the last few years of a policy, but should also take some account of earlier performance which has not been passed on to investors adequately through reversionary bonuses.

    Terminal bonuses can be cut from one year to the next if the markets require it. Bonuses have been cut in recent years, therefore do not expect past returns to be an accurate guide to future payouts.

    As with all life insurance policies the returns will depend on your age, sex and health. Younger, healthier policyholders will get a higher return than a person who is high risk in terms of life insurance.

- *Unit-linked* These policies can either be single premium bonds paid with a lump sum and with a small amount of life cover, or they can be regular premium investments. Unlike with-profits policies which depend on bonuses to iron out rises and falls in the stock markets, unit linked policies are linked directly to the stock market. And while with-profits bonuses cannot be taken away, the value of unit-linked funds can fall (as happened during the stock market crash of 1987).

  As with unit trusts, the investment fund is split into units. These rise and fall in line with the underlying value of the investment fund. However, the risks are spread by investing in a mix of funds.
- *Unitised with-profits* These are a new type of endowment fund which is still a with-profits policy made up of bonuses but with the fund split into units, like a unit-linked fund.
- *Low-cost* This is a more cut-price policy, which guarantees a smaller lump sum and a small bonus. The premiums are much lower than a full endowment.
- *Low-start, low-cost* For the first five years of your policy you pay less in premiums, although they rise by 20 per cent every year and then stay at a higher level thereafter until the end.

Protecting against sickness

There are a number of policies that cover you should you fall ill — permanent health insurance, to cover the day-to-day costs of living if you fall ill; critical illness cover, to provide a lump sum to ease the pain should you fall ill with a serious illness; and private medical insurance, to cover private health care and hospital expenses.

Permanent health insurance

Permanent health insurance is intended to replace your income should you become unable to work due to ill health or disability. There are about 1.4 million policies in force, covering 5 million lives.

Permanent health insurance (PHI) can be taken out by you or your employer. The maximum you can insure for is normally 75 per cent of your earnings, less the State benefits to which you are entitled. PHI cover is written for the long term, usually up to age 60 or 65.

Payments begin after a deferred period so that the insurer can check the validity of your claim. Once payments start your other life and pension premiums should be paid. Beware, some PHI policies do not cover the self-employed. From 5 April 1994 tax will be charged once the benefit has been paid for 12 months.

Critical illness cover

Critical illness cover ensures that you receive a lump sum should you fall seriously ill with a critical illness: cancer, stroke and heart disease are the most common. But other critical illnesses such as permanent disability and renal problems are often covered. Be sure to check exactly what illnesses are covered before taking out a policy.

Obviously the number of illnesses covered and the size of the lump sum you require should you fall ill will determine the size of the premiums.

The lump sum will help you to finance all sorts of things: it could give you a much needed holiday to convalesce, provide you with disability facilities, and generally make your life more comfortable.

Critical illness cover is particularly important for single people with no dependants (more so even than life assurance) but also for couples with small children who depend on them and the self-employed who cannot rely on any financial support from an employer. If critical illness were to strike, not only would a self-employed person lose income in the short term, but also risk losing the business.

Less than 1.5 per cent of the working population holds a policy as the costs tend to be high and these policies are relatively new.

Private medical insurance

Some 3.2 million people in Britain have subscribed to private medical insurance (PMI) schemes, covering nearly 6.5 million people.

More and more organisations are offering their employees PMI as a perk. It is in their interests to do so, as it means that should you fall ill, PMI can usually ensure speedy, comfortable medical treatment, through a private doctor or a private clinic. This is particularly true for minor operations. And you should then be back to work more quickly — an advantage to employers as they will lose less working days through sickness.

Many organisations also extend this cover to a person's spouse and family for a small extra fee. You will be taxed on employer-paid private medical insurance as it is classed as a perk.

Most PMI plans fall into two types: 'full refund' and budget plans.

With the more expensive full refund policies, you should be covered for the cost of a stay in hospital, operation, in-patient treatments like radiotherapy and all your medicines and bandages. But some policies set a limit on the cover or on the amount they will pay out each year.

When you take out a policy, you will normally have to state which band or grade of hospital you want to be treated in. By switching to cheaper hospitals, you can cut the costs.

If you are forced to stay in a higher band hospital you may have to foot some or all of the cost yourself. Even in minor cases you might have to fork out more than £1000.

Most policies do not cover illnesses that you already have and may exclude any condition that you have suffered from in the past five years.

Budget plans are obviously cheaper, but at the same time the cover is also reduced. Usually they will only pay out if you would have to wait more than six weeks to be treated by the NHS.

All policies come with a list of exclusions. You will have to pay if you want to have these conditions treated privately.

Common exclusion clauses include: chronic, incurable conditions; normal pregnancy and childbirth; standard dental and optical treatment; the services of your GP; treatment of AIDS; most types of cosmetic surgery; infertility treatments; conditions caused by dangerous or professional sports; and kidney dialysis.

You can cut your costs further by opting for voluntary excesses with some schemes, but this means that you have to pay the first slice of any claim in return for lower premiums.

People aged over 60 can get tax relief on PMI premiums, and can cut a quarter off the costs. A husband and wife can both get the relief as soon as one partner crosses that age barrier. Tax relief is limited to 25 per cent from 1994/95 (previously a higher rate of relief was available).

Basic rate tax relief is deducted when you pay the premium and higher rate taxpayers receive the extra relief through their tax code or tax assessments.

Tax relief is also available to sons and daughters if they pay the premiums on your behalf and non-taxpayers can also obtain basic rate tax relief. But some policies do not qualify under Inland Revenue rules, usually because they offer cash benefits.

Small print

Don't just look at the cost of health insurance. Remember you get what you pay for and a cheaper price may also mean less cover.

Increasingly patients are finding that they have to pick up part — or even all — of health care bills themselves because they have failed to read the small print.

Certain types of treatment and even hospitals may be excluded from cover and some consultants have even been blacklisted for overcharging. Insurers now recommend — and often insist — that patients check that their treatment will be covered in advance.

In some cases there may be a limit. Some insurers have now imposed limits on the amount they will pay for various operations and treatments. This can leave patients with a bill for treatment — even though they already have cover. And in some cases patients have had treatment only to find that their complaint is excluded.

£ ——————————————————————————————— £
Money tips

Check the following:
- Ask about existing conditions and if they are excluded.
- Is there cover outside the UK?
- Is the choice of hospital restricted?
- Are there limits on cover?
- Do you have to wait for treatment?
- Is there a policy excess?
- Can you get second opinions?
- Is there a limit on how long you can stay in hospital?
- Are outpatient services covered and if so are there restrictions or limits on what can be spent?
- Is there a cash benefit if you opt for the NHS instead of using your private healthcare?

£ ——————————————————————————————— £

Protecting your income

There is no point in building up a nest egg only to have to spend it on day-to-day living because you suffer from a drop in income or cannot work due to illness.

You can protect your income through insurance. This is particularly important if you are self-employed, rely on commission to boost your income or do not qualify for State benefits.

Policies include the following.

Credit insurance

Credit insurance can be bought with your loan, storecard or mortgage. It is known as payment protection. You may have it without realising it as it was common for those taking out loans to tick a box on the application form if they did *not* want cover.

Income protection plans

An income protection plan is an insurance taken out to provide an income should you be made redundant. The period of cover depends on the policy and there is often a set period before payments are made. Ask your bank, lender or mortgage company for details if you want to protect your borrowing, or an insurance broker if you want a general policy.

Legal expenses insurance

Legal expenses insurance covers the solicitors' and barristers' fees when you decide to take someone or some organisation to court, and other legal expenses including the other party's costs should you lose. Cover is normally up to £25,000 or £50,000 per claim.

At least 7.5 million people have legal expenses insurance cover.

There are two ways of buying legal expenses insurance: the first, as an add-on to your car or household insurance, is fairly cheap. In the case of a car accident it allows you to sue to recover your excess, your loss of earnings, or the cost of hiring a car.

If this type of insurance is added to your household insurance, it will enable you to take out civil actions relating to the house, employment disputes, personal injury, or allow you to defend minor motoring offences.

Buying a separate legal protection policy is far more expensive and you can pay anything from £15 to £50 a year depending on the amount of cover you think you require. The policies will cover you for most disputes, unless the insurance companies don't think you can win.

Generally policies vary considerably in content but should give you cover for: consumer disputes, personal injury claims, inheritance disputes, employment difficulties, motor claims, and many other legal disputes. You can often buy legal expenses insurance as an addition to motor or household cover at a cheaper rate than a separate policy.

Most policies provide policyholders with free legal advice by a 24-hour telephone service.

Travel insurance

A holiday 'package' insurance policy includes cover against a number of different eventualities such as cancellation, delay, personal accident, personal liability, medical expenses and loss or damage to property.

Policies are fairly inexpensive, around £20 per adult for a fortnight's cover in Europe.

Package policies may not be suitable for everyone, and it is possible to arrange 'selective' policies, where you can choose the type and amount of cover you need. Most policies are arranged through the travel agent or tour operator selling the holiday.

One person in fifteen will eventually make a claim on a travel policy. Around half of these are for cancellation, a further quarter for medical expenses and the majority of the rest for loss of belongings.

£ ——————————————————————— £
Money tips

The amount of cover can vary widely between travel insurance policies and you could find yourself underinsured. Take note of these tips. You need:

- At least £1500 cover for your belongings. The policy should cover you for up to £100 to buy emergency supplies if your baggage is delayed when flying.
- Enough cover for the money that you are taking with you. The limit for money is usually about £500, but there is often a separate amount for cash. Companies sometimes define money as cash, others as traveller's cheques. So make sure you check this out before you agree to travel insurance.
- Adequate medical expenses cover: £250,000 for Europe; and £1 million for the US and the rest of the world.
- Cover for the full cost of your holiday — just in case you have to cut your trip short (this includes the deposit and any other charges that you have paid in advance).
- £1 million personal liability cover in Europe and the rest of the world, and at least £2 million in the US.
£ ——————————————————————— £

6

Making the most of your mortgage

Buying a home is one of the biggest financial commitments you are likely ever to make in your life. You are agreeing to borrow £30,000, £60,000 or even £100,000 and to keep up the repayments on this month in and month out for 25 years or more.

But while you may spend weeks — if not months or years — picking the home of your dreams, often very little thought goes into the finances of buying a home.

Yet by picking the wrong lender — or wrong type of mortgage — you could lose substantially over the long run. Every homebuyer — whether you are a first-time buyer, moving up the property ladder or an existing borrower looking to cut your outgoings by remortgaging — should put their mortgage at the top of their list of financial priorities.

Picking a mortgage

What type of mortgage

A mortgage is a legal charge over a property as security for a loan. There are several types, described below.

Repayment

A repayment mortgage involves borrowing for a fixed term (usually 25 years). Monthly repayments cover the interest on the loan and an element towards paying off the capital.

At the beginning of the mortgage you will be paying off mainly interest and only a little of the capital. This gradually changes so that at the end of the term your payments are mostly reducing the capital. So if you repay your mortgage after just a few years, you will have only repaid a small amount of the loan.

Most lenders recommend that you also take out a life insurance policy to cover the loan should you die. The cheapest is called term insurance or assurance. This runs for the term of the loan and is much cheaper than an endowment policy. However, unlike an endowment policy there is no investment element so you get nothing back if you survive until the end of the term. The policies are also called mortgage protection plans.

Repayment mortgages can be flexible. If you are having difficulty making repayments, your lender will probably allow you to reduce your monthly repayments by extending the mortgage term up to 25 years. Most lenders do not extend the term beyond 25 years. Or you may be allowed to make interest-only repayments for a while.

- *Advantages* You can see the amount you borrow reducing each year. The costs can be cheaper if your endowment premiums are expensive because you are a higher risk for life assurance.
- *Disadvantages* However, when your loan is reduced to less than £30,000 you no longer get the maximum amount of mortgage interest tax relief (MITR). (MITR is paid on the first £30,000). Also you do not get a lump sum when the loan is repaid as you can from an endowment, pension or PEP mortgage.

Endowment

An endowment mortgage is an interest-only loan. This means that your monthly payments cover only the interest on the loan. Nothing goes towards repaying the initial amount borrowed. Then at the end of the term (usually 25 years) the debt is repaid by the endowment policy.

Every month, in addition to the interest, you pay an insurance premium into the endowment policy. When this matures it should repay the loan and give an additional lump sum (however, this is not guaranteed).

An endowment policy is a life insurance contract. It includes an element of life insurance cover — to repay the loan should you die — but is more of an investment. The money is invested in a mix of shares, British Government stocks and property. The costs of running these policies mean that they are only normally suitable as investments for 10 years or more.

CHOOSE A MORTGAGE THAT SUITS *YOUR* NEEDS

The PEP Mortgage Company can find you a top quality mortgage and a repayment method which is:

- **Cheaper**
- **Flexible**
- **Tax Free**

Typically, you could save up to £50 a month by using a PEP to repay your loan instead of an endowment.

All the usual mortgages are available - fixed term loans, discounts - at highly competitive rates from highly competitive lenders.

A PEP Mortgage gives you the flexibility to:

- **Repay the loan early.**
- **Make use of a tax free fund.**
- **Vary your premiums.**

The cost effective charging structure in a PEP means that more of your money is actually working to pay off the loan *from day one.*

Our advice is without obligation - for details of current offers simply give us a call..

**The PEP Mortgage Company Limited
16 St John Street
LONDON
EC1M 4AY
Tel: 071 454 9320; Fax 071 454 9453**

Your home is at risk if you do not keep up repayments on a mortgage or other loan secured on it.

- *Advantages* Some of the cheaper mortgages are only offered on an endowment basis so you may be able to get a cheaper rate. You may get a lump sum in addition to repaying your loan at the end of the mortgage term. This makes these schemes a good choice for those who would not save in any other way.
- *Disadvantages* If you cash in your endowment early you may get little or nothing back on your investment as the costs of setting up these policies are quite high. If you are older and a smoker your endowment premiums may be higher because the life insurance element of your endowment will cost more, to reflect the higher risk of a claim being made.
- *The pros and cons of cashing in an endowment policy* Seven in 10 life insurance policies are cashed in early even though investors are warned not to surrender if they are strapped for cash. It is far better to keep paying the premiums and reap the full benefits when your endowment policy matures.

However, thousands of hard-pressed homebuyers have had to surrender their endowments because they cannot afford the premiums. And for many others — particularly those caught with mortgages worth more than their homes or in need of a lump sum — cashing in an endowment early can pay off. Nevertheless, early surrender is not a good recommendation overall.

Warning

Weigh up all the financial options before surrendering, and seek financial advice.

When weighing up the financial consequences of surrendering an endowment policy, consider the following:

- It only makes sense if you do not need to use the policy to back another mortgage.
- Ask your life insurance company for the surrender value of your policy and how much you have paid in premiums over the years. That way, if it looks a very unattractive option, you can decide not to go ahead.
- Look at alternatives: suspending payments for a while or reducing them, selling the policy to a third party or auctioning it. For names and addresses of firms that buy endowments contact: The Association of Policy Market Makers, Fullbridge Mill, Maldon, Essex, CM9 7FN. Tel: 071-813 1483.
- You may also be able to borrow against your endowment policy to raise some extra cash.
- Beware of advisers who try to tempt you to set up other investment plans instead; they might wrongly advise you to surrender your existing policy simply so you can open an new one with them.
- If your policy was taken out before 1984, there will probably be tax relief on the premiums which you will never be able to benefit from again if you take out a new policy.

Pension

A pension mortgage uses a tax efficient pension scheme to repay the loan instead of an endowment. The mortgage is interest-only but instead of paying into an endowment policy your money goes into a pension scheme. The advantage of this is that you get tax relief on your top rate of tax in a pension scheme. So basic rate taxpayers get 25p from the Inland Revenue for every 75p they invest and higher rate taxpayers get 40p for every 60p. As personal pensions can be taken from age 50 there is no need for you to retire to repay your mortgage.

Again it is recommended that you take out life insurance cover. But as this can be purchased through the pension plan with its tax breaks it is cheaper than other forms of life insurance cover.

- *Advantages* This is an excellent tax break as not only does your money grow free of tax, you also get tax relief. This makes pension mortgages more suitable for higher rate taxpayers. These schemes give the highest potential payout over the long run.
- *Disadvantages* If you are in a company pension scheme you cannot take out a personal pension plan as well. Pension mortgages are therefore mainly suitable for the self-employed and those not in a company scheme. If you use your pension to pay off your mortgage you will have less to retire on unless you fund it adequately. If you lose your job and cease to be a taxpayer you will not get tax relief on your contributions. You cannot get hold of your investments until you reach 50 at the earliest.

PEP

A PEP mortgage uses another tax efficient investment scheme — a Personal Equity Plan — to repay the mortgage. This is similar to an endowment in that the money is usually invested in a fund such as a unit trust. But the tax breaks mean that the cash can grow tax free.

If the investment performs well, there will be no need to wait 25 years to repay your mortgage as it can be cashed in early. Again you will be advised to take out separate life insurance cover.

- *Advantages* The investment returns should be good over the long run, enabling the homebuyer to repay the mortgage early. If your investments perform well you can cash them in whenever you like — free of tax.
- *Disadvantages* You will probably pay more into your PEP than into an endowment and the risks are higher. If the stockmarket crashes as you are coming up to repay your mortgage your investment could almost halve overnight.

What type of mortgage is best for me?

Debate has been growing on the merits of endowment vs repayment mortgages. More than seven in ten new mortgages are endowment schemes. However, as they earn lenders commission there has been criticism that they are being sold to some borrowers even though a repayment mortgage may be a better choice. At the same time many life insurance companies have reduced the payouts of their endowment policies.

Nevertheless, endowments still produce good returns and are suitable for many homebuyers. Seek advice before taking out a mortgage.

Picking the right endowment policy is essential if you pick an endowment mortgage, as the difference in the payout between the best and worst policies can be 50 per cent or more.

However, increasingly borrowers are given little choice as to which endowment they must buy. Most lenders are tied to one life insurance company, which means they can sell only that company's policies, or they may own their own life company.

Endowments are more investments than life insurance and contracts can be bought for any term over 10 years. The usual term for an endowment mortgage is 25 years.

Endowments can be low-start or low-cost which cuts the costs, and they can be in joint names.

There are three basic types: with-profits, unit-linked and unitised with-profits (see Chapter 5 for more on life assurance).

One thing you must do before you choose a mortgage is to compare the monthly costs and take into account any endowment premium or pension contribution (on a pension mortgage), that you will have to pay. With all mortgages except endowments you should include a mortgage protection policy.

How the costs vary

Some loans are better bets when rates are lower (see table 3).

TABLE 3

Monthly costs of loan taken out by male aged 29 who is a non-smoker over 25 years including life insurance premium.

£30,000 at 8% average rate mortgage + investment/life cover		£60,000 at 8% average rate mortgage + investment/life cover	
Endowment:	£150.00 + £42.84 endowment premium	£350.00 + £84.88 endowment premium	
Repayment:	£195.57 + £5.80 mortgage protection	£418.40 + £10.60 mortgage protection	

Pension:	£150.00 + £37.86 pension + £8.10 life cover	£350.00 + £75.16 pension + £16.20 life cover
PEP:	£150.00 + £50 PEP £7.00 life cover	£350.00 + £78.24 PEP + £13.00 life cover
£30,000 at 12% average rate mortgage + investment/life cover		**£60,000 at 12% average rate mortgage + investment/life cover**
Endowment:	£225.00 + £42.84 endowment premium	£525.00 + £84.88 endowment premium
Repayment:	£254.52 + £5.80 mortgage protection	£562.50 + £10.60 mortgage protection
Pension:	£225.00 + £37.86 pension + £8.10 life cover	£525.00 + £75.16 pension + £16.20 life cover
PEP:	£225.00 + £50 PEP + £7.00 life cover	£525.00 + £78.24 PEP + £13.00 life cover

Source: Halifax Building Society

Fixed or variable?

Most mortgages are variable-rate loans which means that the interest you pay rises and falls with interest rates. Over the long run the average mortgage rate has been between 10 per cent and 12 per cent, but at some times it has risen to as much as 15.4 per cent and fallen to less than 8 per cent. It means that borrowers run the risk of very high repayments.

Four in ten loans are adjusted annually rather than with each move in interest rates; these are known as annual review mortgages. The amount of interest charged changes as interest rates rise and fall but the repayments only vary once a year. The aim of these schemes is to allow homebuyers to budget for the year ahead.

The other alternative is a fixed-rate loan which has repayments set on a fixed rate of interest over a set period. Fixed-rate mortgages have become increasingly popular as interest rates have fallen. When rates are low it makes sense to tie in to them. However, most fixed-rate loans are only for one, two or five years. Very few are for the full 25 years.

Fixed-rate mortgages allow you to budget: your repayments will not be affected by fluctuations in interest rates during the fixed period. But remember that your repayments could rise sharply if rates are high when the fixed rate ends. Also bear in mind that you will not benefit if interest rates fall during the fixed-rate period.

What if I want to redeem a fixed-rate mortgage?

Choosing the length of a fixed-rate mortgage can be difficult, as you need to balance the security of fixed repayments against the costs you would incur if you repaid the mortgage within the fixed period. Fixed-rate mortgages usually have high penalties — three month's interest is typical — if you want to revert to the variable rate. Most lenders allow you to take a fixed-rate mortgage with you when you sell and move within the UK.

Most lenders make a charge of between £200 and £300 for arranging a fixed-rate mortgage, on top of the normal mortgage costs.

Other types of mortgages

Homebuyers can also take out 'capped' rate mortgages which guarantee that the loan rate will not rise above a certain level for a set period of time. But at the same time, borrowers can benefit from rate cuts.

'Cap and collar' mortgages are similar, but in addition to an upper level ('cap') there is a lower level — known as a 'collar' — below which the loan rate will not fall.

Low-start mortgages — with reduced costs in the initial years of the loan — are also available.

How to compare the cost of different mortgages

Don't just look at the headline mortgage rate — look at the APR (annual percentage rate). The APR provides a better idea of the true cost of borrowing than the interest rate alone.

Many mortgages offer an initial discount which cuts the rate in the first few months or years. But the APR will show how much they cost over the long run. They can work out more expensive than a standard variable-rate loan because arrangement fees are added.

As can be seen from Table 4, the loan that looks the cheapest may not work out that way in the long run.

TABLE 4 TOTAL TWO-YEAR COST OF DIFFERENT RATE LOANS

£50,000 loan fixed at 8.0% for 2 years then variable.
Comes with a £350 arrangement fee.
TOTAL COST: £8,517.92.

£50,000 loan variable rate — currently 7.5% but rises to 8% in six months
and then 9% six months later.
TOTAL COST: £8,418.96.

£50,000 loan with a 1% discount for 1 year bringing rate down to 6.5% —
then rises to 9%. Comes with a £500 arrangement fee.
TOTAL COST: £8,527.04.

Should I repay my loan early?

Mortgages are one of the cheapest ways to borrow over the long run
because of tax relief. Although this has been reduced to 20 per cent
from April 1994 it still cuts the cost of borrowing considerably.

On a £30,000 loan (the maximum that qualifies for MITR) a loan rate
of 10 per cent works out at just 8 per cent after tax relief. From
1995/96 the tax relief will be cut to 15 per cent.

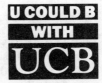

Depending on investment returns it can pay to put your money to work in a high-paying savings account or investment scheme rather than repay your loan (which is declining in real terms every year thanks to inflation). Or you could use some of the money to boost your pension and get tax relief to increase it by a further 25 per cent or 40 per cent, depending on your rate of tax.

However, many borrowers who find themselves with a lump sum prefer to pay off their mortgage because it gives them a feeling of security and peace of mind.

Paying off your mortgage early by making larger monthly payments or reducing the term could save you thousands of pounds in interest — and leave you debt free.

You can cut your home loan down to size either by paying off a lump sum or by making regular additional payments.

A borrower with a £60,000 home loan would be a massive £15,200 better off by repaying over 20 years instead of 25, assuming interest rates of 7.99 per cent.

As interest rates have come down, more people can afford to pay extra off their mortgage.

If you pay off an endowment mortgage, try to keep your policy going for the full term. Returns will be cut if you cash in early. Repayment mortgages are more flexible.

Warning

If you pay more in monthly mortgage payments in order to reduce your loan you could be losing out. Some lenders do not credit these extra payments until the end of the charging year and in the meantime do not give you interest.

You are better off investing these extra payments in a high-interest account and then repaying part of the loan when you have enough to make a one-off payment.

Take care before you pay anything off a fixed rate loan — you could be charged 90 days' penalty interest or even more.

The amount that lenders will agree to accept as a lump-sum repayment varies between £100 and £1000. If you have a fixed-term loan or a discount mortgage you may suffer penalties for making any lump sum repayments, however small. Check with your lender first.

Which lender?

Mortgages are offered by building societies, banks, finance houses, insurance companies and specialised mortgage companies. Tables are produced which show the cheapest and most expensive mortgage lenders over the long run. But this is no guarantee that these lenders will be cheaper in the future.

Generally banks and specialised mortgage companies tend to be cheaper when rates are low and more expensive when they are high. This is because, unlike building societies, they do not have savers to consider; when rates hit a very low level, there is a limit to how low savers' rates can go. But in contrast, when rates are high the building societies have been able to reduce the impact on their borrowers.

What if I want to change my mortgage?

If you want to switch to a cheaper-rate mortgage or increase your loan you can remortgage. Watch out for loss of MIRAS — mortgage interest relief at source — if you are a joint buyer and currently qualify for two lots of £30,000 tax relief. Also watch out for extra costs such as valuation fees and legal costs. You will also lose tax relief on home improvement loans if you remortgage.

What affects the price of my mortgage?

The riskier a lending proposition you are considered to be, the higher the rate you are likely to be charged. A few lenders still offer mortgages to those with little or no deposit, to the self-employed who cannot 'prove' their income and to those wanting to borrow more than three times their salary. But these riskier loans tend to come at a price. Increasingly lenders are offering cheaper rates to those borrowers with a substantial deposit, which often has to be 25 per cent of the value of the property.

How much can I borrow?

There are two things that dictate how much you can borrow.

The first is the loan to value percentage — the loan as a percentage of the value of the property. This is often restricted to 95 per cent of the property's value. So if you are buying a £100,000 house you can have a mortgage of up to £95,000; or on a £50,000 home, a loan of up to £47,500.

The rest of the money must be made up with a deposit. Lenders often require 10 to 20 per cent deposits to qualify for the cheapest loans.

The second factor is your income. The income multiple is generally 3 × salary. If there are joint buyers this is restricted to 3 × the first salary plus the second, or 2.5 × joint income.

So if one partner earns £20,000 a year and the other £10,000 they can borrow either:

- 3 × £20,000 = £60,000 + 1 × £10,000 = £70,000, or:
- 2.5 × £30,000 (£20,000 + £10,000) = £75,000.

If you are self-employed you will normally be required to give the lender three years' accounts to prove your income. More restrictive lending policies mean that some lenders now limit loans available to those who make up some of their income from commission or over-time, which may not be included in the salary multiples.

If you have insufficient income to support the loan requested, the lender may insist on a guarantor who will guarantee to repay the loan if you (the borrower) default.

How much should I borrow?

Never borrow more than you can afford. Remember that interest rates can rise and your mortgage bills could double from their present level at certain times during the term of your loan. Assume that interest rates average between 10 per cent and 12 per cent to calculate whether or not you can afford your mortgage (see Table 3 for repayments at different interest rates).

Never rely on income you hope to get such as a Christmas bonus — it may not be forthcoming. Lenders have been hit by record levels of mortgage arrears and repossessions, so are unlikely to let you borrow more than you can afford, but you should still ensure that you can afford to repay what you borrow.

Work out a monthly budget of outgoings including other loans — and loans you plan to take out to cover the costs of moving, new furniture, carpets, kitchens etc. In total, these borrowing costs should not add up to more than about half your monthly income to allow for rises in the cost of borrowing.

There are also other costs known as disbursements, which include

Land Registry fees, solicitors' fees, stamp duty and local authority search fees. Stamp duty is currently charged at 1 per cent of the purchase price on any property costing £60,000 or more. You can use Table 5 to calculate your moving costs.

TABLE 5 CALCULATING YOUR COSTS

Buying	*Estimated cost £*
Stamp duty	
Solicitor's fees	
Searches	
Land Registry (registered property)	
Solicitor's disbursements	
Lending source's solicitor's fees	
Mortgage indemnity guarantee	
Lender's valuation	
Survey fee	
Buildings insurance	
Removal firm	
TOTAL COSTS	
Selling — if you are selling as well you will need to add on:	*Estimated cost £*
Solicitor's fees for the sale	
Estate agency sale fee	
TOTAL COSTS	

TABLE 6 COSTS OF BUYING AND SELLING

England and Wales

House price	Cost of selling		Cost of buying	
£50,000	Solicitor	£287	Solicitor	£298
	Estate agent	£1367	Land Registry	£100
	Removals	£213	Searches	£58
			Stamp duty	nil
	TOTAL	£1867	Home purchase report	£225
			Removals	£213
			TOTAL	£894

House price £100,000	Cost of selling		Cost of buying	
	Solicitor	£385	Solicitor	£403
	Estate agent	£2700	Land Registry	£230
	Removals	£313	Searches	£58
			Stamp duty	£1000
	TOTAL	£3398	Home purchase report	£325
			Removals	£313
			TOTAL	£2329

Scotland

House price £50,000	Cost of selling		Cost of buying	
	Solicitor	£536	Solicitor	£562
	Estate agent	£588	Recording dues	£132
	Cost of title search P16		Stamp duty	Nil
	Report	£53	Home purchase report	£225
	Enquiries	£77	Removals	£149
	Dues of discharge	£48	TOTAL	£1038
	Miscellaneous	£85		
	Removals	£149		
	TOTAL	£1536		

£100,000	Solicitor	£837	Solicitor	£992
	Estate agent	£1151	Recording dues	£242
	Cost of title search P16		Stamp duty	£1000
	Report	£53	Home purchase report	£325
	Enquiries	£77	Removals	£251
	Dues of discharge	£97	TOTAL	£2810
	Miscellaneous	£89		
	Removals	£251		
	TOTAL	£2555		

(Source: Woolwich Building Society's *Moving Report*, 1993)

Table 6 will give you a good overall idea of what the total costs of buying and selling a house in England and Wales or Scotland are likely to be.

Do I have to borrow over 25 years?

You can take a mortgage out for just 10 years if you prefer. Monthly interest costs will not increase as a result.

However, if you are hoping to repay your loan with an endowment you will find that the extra premiums you will have to pay will push up the costs of the loan considerably.

Repayment mortgages do cost more if the term is reduced to a shorter period. The cost of a reducing a £30,000 repayment mortgage from 25 to 20 years is only about £22 a month.

If the term of a 25-year mortgage takes you past retirement age you may be required to take out a shorter-term mortgage so that you are not left with monthly mortgage bills to pay after retirement — although this is not as relevant nowadays as it used to be.

Mortgage indemnity

Mortgage indemnity insurance covers the loan against default. So if you fail to keep up repayments and the property is repossessed the lender can claim some of its losses back from the insurance policy.

This protects the lender — not the borrower — yet it is the borrower who must pay. Some lenders do not operate this type of scheme and others own their own insurance company to protect against default. But generally, most lenders require a borrower to take out a mortgage indemnity policy. This allows a borrower to borrow more than the 'normal lending limits'.

How much does it cost?

The cost depends on how much you want to borrow. Generally you must pay for mortgage indemnity insurance if you want to borrow more than 70 per cent or 75 per cent of the value of the property. This is defined as the 'normal lending limits'.

At the time of writing the costs were 7 per cent of the difference between the threshold and the loan value for mortgages up to 95 per cent. This means that the borrower pays a premium of 7 per cent of the difference between the loan size (say 95 per cent) and the point at which indemnity must be paid (say 75 per cent). On a £100,000 loan this works out at 7 per cent of £20,000 (£95,000 – £75,000) ie £1400.

How are properties valued?

A house may be on the market for a price that you are prepared to pay, but that does not necessarily mean that you can get a mortgage for that amount. This is because valuations are based on a number of factors, including the price the property would fetch if it had to be sold quickly.

The cost of a valuation depends on the purchase price of the property. Sometimes known as a Building Society Valuation Report, it is not an in-depth survey. It is only designed for mortgage purposes, and the value shown takes no account of any carpets or fittings in the purchase price. Nor does a valuation report guarantee that the property is free from defects.

So if you have any doubts about the fabric of the property you intend to buy and aspects like subsidence, damp and the wiring and plumbing, you should opt for a more detailed Home Buyer's Report or (if you can afford it) have a full structural survey done.

The Home Buyer's Report provides general information on the quality and condition of the property, inside and out. The full structural survey is the most comprehensive report available and gives you a complete breakdown on each part of the structure, highlighting any defects. This is especially worth it if you are buying an old property or one that needs renovation.

Is leasehold better than freehold?

Buying freehold gives the homebuyer indefinite ownership of the land. Leasehold restricts ownership to the term of the lease. When the lease expires the buyer is left with nothing. However, if you buy a flat it will be leasehold, not freehold, as freehold flats cannot be purchased; however, you can buy a freehold separately.

Leaseholders are often given the opportunity to extend their lease and the new Leasehold Reform Act gives many the right to purchase the freehold at the market price.

Mortgages on short leases are hard to get, but you should be able to get a loan provided the lease has at least another 20 years or so to run after the mortgage has been completely repaid (eg if the mortgage term is 25 years, the lease will probably need to have at least 45 years to run).

What are the tax breaks in home buying?

MITR — Mortgage Interest Tax Relief — is the tax relief given to home-buyers. It makes a mortgage one of the cheapest ways to borrow money.

Most mortgage repayments are calculated to include MIRAS (Mortgage Interest Relief At Source) but very occasionally homebuyers have to reclaim the tax relief through their tax coding because their lender is not part of the scheme.

Only the first £30,000 of a mortgage on the purchase of your principal private property qualifies. Interest on the portion of the loan over £30,000 is paid in full.

Home improvement loans are excluded unless they were made before 6 April 1988.

Since 6 April 1991 higher rate tax relief has not been available. And from 6 April 1994 tax relief will only be given at the 20 per cent rate, not the 25 per cent basic tax rate. But it still means homebuyers will only pay £800 for every £1000 of gross interest on the first £30,000 of the loan. The reduced rate of 20 per cent will not apply to loans to the over-65s to buy a life annuity. From 1995/96 the relief will be cut further to 15 per cent.

MITR is not available if more than a third of your home is let or used for business purposes.

Non-tax payers still qualify for MIRAS.

Joint homebuyers no longer get two lots of MITR as it is restricted to £30,000 per property for loans made after August 1988.

Unmarried home sharers can still each claim interest relief on a loan up to £30,000 if the loan was made before 1 August 1988, giving them £60,000 of tax relief. However, married couples only qualify for £30,000 of MITR between them.

The other tax break when buying your home is that no capital gains tax (CGT) is paid when you sell your principal private residence. However, if you have let the property out you may have to pay CGT (ask your local Inland Revenue Enquiry Centre for advice).

In addition, the profits made on your endowment policy are tax free.

What if I own a second home?

You will not get MITR on the loan on a second home and will be liable for CGT when you sell it. Also watch out for difficulties in insuring a home left empty for most of the week or let out for holiday accomodation.

7
How to reduce your tax bill

Up to 30 million people are paying too much tax — that is almost three in four of the adult population. If everyone got on top of their tax affairs they could save some £8 billion in tax, according to IFA Promotion, the organisation which represents independent financial advisers. IFA recently undertook a study which found that £4.1 billion of tax was easily avoidable or paid in error. Some £1 billion of this should never have been paid or can be claimed back.

Understanding your tax position

Tax is paid at different rates and not all your income is taxed. To make the most of your money you will need to undertand the basics of national insurance, income tax, capital gains and inheritance tax and the tax position of savings and investments. Then you can get to grips with ways to minimise your tax, claim tax relief and get tax back.

Income tax

Income tax is a tax on income. It is split into schedules. There are, however, allowances and deductions that enable you to cut your tax bill.

Everyone has to pay income tax on income above tax thresholds. However, a child's income may be treated as a parent's if it comes from the parent. And before 6 April 1990 a married woman's income was normally treated as her husband's income.

The income tax year runs from 6 April in one year to 5 April in the next, but the income charged to tax in any tax year is not always the amount arising during that tax year because of the different rules for measuring different types of income. These are known as schedules and cases. The main ones are listed in Table 7.

TABLE 7 TAX SCHEDULES

Schedule and case	Type of income	Basis of assessment	Normal due date of payment
Schedule A	Rents from UK land and buildings	Rent due in tax year, less allowable expenses	1 January in tax year
Schedule C	Income from UK and foreign government stocks, paid through UK paying agent such as a bank	Income received in tax year	Basic rate tax deducted by payer and accounted for to the Revenue; excess over basic rate due 1 December in next tax year
Schedule D			
Case I	Profits of trade }	Normally profits of accounting year ending in previous tax year	Equal instalments on 1 January in tax year and 1 July following
Case II	Profits of profession } or vocation }		
Case III	Interest, annuities or other annual amounts received	Income received in tax year where tax is deducted by the payer or where interest is received gross from a building society or bank (other than the National Savings Bank)	As for Schedule C if tax is deducted at source, otherwise 1 January
Case IV	Income from foreign securities }	Normally amount arising in previous tax year	Normally 1 January in year of assessment
Case V	Income from foreign possessions }		

Schedule and case	Type of income	Basis of assessment	Normal due date of payment
Case VI	Income not assessable under any other schedule or case	Profits or gains arising in tax year, less appropriate expenses	1 January in tax year
Schedule E Case I	Earnings of employee resident and ordinarily resident in UK, other than 'foreign emoluments' earned wholly abroad	All earnings in the tax year whether duties are performed in the UK or abroad	Normally under PAYE system, otherwise 30 days after issue of of assessment

Tax codes and allowances

Table 8 shows the tax allowances and Table 9 the tax rates which currently apply.

TABLE 8 TAX ALLOWANCES

Personal allowances – the amount you can earn before paying tax.

	1993/94 £	1994/95 £
Basic personal allowance under 65	3,445	3,445
age 65–74	4,200	4,200
75 and over	4,370	4,370
Additional married couple's allowance under 65	1,720	1,720*
age 65–74	2,465	2,668*
75 and over	2,505	2,705*
Additional personal allowance	1,720	1,720*
Widow's bereavement allowance	1,720	1,720
Blind person's allowance	1,080	1,200
Income for age-related allowance	14,200	14,200

*Relief restricted to 20% in 1994/95 and 15% in 1995/96

TABLE 9 TAX RATES 1993/94   **1994/95**

Rate	Charged on taxable earnings	
20 per cent	up to £2,500	up to £3,000
25 per cent	£2,500–£23,700	£3,001–£23,700
40 per cent	£23,700 and over	over £23,700

If you work for an employer you will probably be taxed under the Pay As You Earn (PAYE) system, where tax is deducted from your salary each month, so that you don't have to pay a big bill at the end of the year.

Your PAYE code is made up of a series of numbers and a final letter. This shows how much tax-free pay you are allowed in the whole tax year — and occasionally may show that you cannot earn any income tax free but instead owe the Inland Revenue.

The numbers relate to your allowance (see table 8); if your tax code is 344L, for instance, that means you have £3445 of tax-free pay. The letter tells you which personal allowance you receive (see Table 10).

TABLE 10 Tax code suffix letters

L	You get the basic personal allowance of £3445.
H	You get the personal allowance of £3445 and the married couple's allowance of £1720. This can now be split equally between husband and wife or the whole amount claimed by one.
P	You get the higher single person's allowance of £4200 for those aged between 65 and 74.
V	You get the higher personal allowance for those aged between 65 and 74 and the higher married couple's allowance of £2465.
T	You are given a T code if: your age-related allowance is reduced because your income is more than the £14,200 limit; you are 75 and over during the tax year and get the higher age allowance of £4370 for a single person and £2505 for a married couple; you don't want your employer to know your age or marital status.
K	You get the K code if the value of any perks of your job is greater than your personal allowances. The extra tax will be collected each month through PAYE, so you won't have to pay a big bill at the end of the year.
NT	You pay no tax on this income.
BR	All your earnings are taxed at the basic rate. You might get this code on earnings for a second job.
DO	All your earnings are taxed at the higher rate. You might get this code on earnings from a second job if your main job already puts you into the higher-rate tax bracket.

You should check your tax code is correct and challenge it if you feel there has been an error — for instance, if you no longer have a second income.

If you are over 65 make sure you get your higher personal allowance of £4200 and the higher married couple's allowance of £2465 (£2,665 from the 1994/95 tax year). For those over 75 the allowances rise to £4370 and £2505 (figures refer to 1993–94).

If your total income is more than than £14,200 your age-related allowances are cut by £1 for every £2 by which you exceed the limit. So keep taxable income down with tax-free investments like TESSAs or PEPs.

What is taxed and what is not?

Some income is not taxable — in addition to income up to your tax allowance. See Table 11 for details of the tax position on state benefits.

TABLE 11 MAIN STATE BENEFITS

Taxable	Exempt
Retirement pensions	Wounds or disability pensions
Widow's pension and widowed mother's allowance	War widow's pension
Statutory sick pay	Disability living allowance
Statutory maternity pay	Maternity allowance
Industrial death benefit paid as pension	Widow's payment
Job release allowance for periods beginning earlier than 1 year before pension age	Job release allowance to men aged 64 or over or women aged 59 or over
Income support to unemployed	Child benefit and allowances
Income support to strikers	Attendance allowance
Unemployment benefit	Sickness benefit
Invalid care allowance	Severe disablement allowance
	Family credit
	Housing benefit
	Income support (other than as listed as taxable)
	Christmas bonus for pensioners
	Industrial injury benefits

Other Income

Certain other types of income are exempt including:

- the first £70 of interest from National Savings Bank ordinary accounts;
- increase in value of National Savings certificates;
- premium bond prizes;
- bonuses and profits on life assurance policies;
- prizes and betting winnings;
- Save As You Earn account bonuses;
- shares allocated to you by your employer under an approved profit-sharing scheme;
- profit-related pay, up to a maximum of £4000;
- local authority home improvement grants;
- educational grants and scholarships;
- statutory redundancy pay, pay in lieu of notice and certain larger amounts received from your employer;
- maintenance payments under arrangements made after 14 March 1988, and first £1720 (for 1993/94) of maintenance payments under earlier arrangements.

Tax and your job

PAYE is the usual scheme for employees and directors who are charged tax under Schedule E.

Employees do not receive a tax bill or refund from the Inland Revenue unless there is a significant under or overpayment. Employers deduct tax and national insurance contributions from weekly or monthly pay, using tables supplied by the Inland Revenue.

The tax calculation is made using code numbers supplied by the Inland Revenue.

All directors and employees earning £8500 a year or more are classed as P11D employee (Form P11D is the form employers complete for such employees at the financial year end), and this means that they are taxed not only on cash pay but also on cash equivalent benefits in kind.

Full-time directors earning less than £8500 are not P11D employees, unless they own more than 5 per cent of the ordinary share capital. If you are not a P11D employee, you are not normally taxed on benefits unless they can be turned into cash.

If you use your own car for business, you can claim the business proportion of the running expenses (calculated on a mileage basis), capital allowances, and relief for interest on a loan to buy a car. If your employer pays you a mileage allowance, this will be taxable. However, your employer can obtain a dispensation from the Inland Revenue to enable the mileage allowance to be ignored, and you then have to make an expenses claim.

If you need to work from home you will be able to claim a proportion of the cost of light, heat, telephone, etc. If you use a room exclusively for work, a proportion of your council tax is allowed as well.

There are ways to cut tax on your pay. Profit-related pay of up to £4000 or a fifth of your pay — whichever is the lower — can be paid tax free each year if you are in approved schemes. Save As You Earn share option schemes are also tax free and payments of up to £5000 for staff suggestions are also tax free.

Tax on perks

Company cars

The tax on company cars is changing. If you do not use your car for business and it is purely a perk, it may pay you to opt for a salary rise instead.

If you do more than 18,000 business miles a year in your company car, the scale charge is halved. If you do fewer than 2500, however, it is increased by 50 per cent — but the fuel scale charge is not increased. This came into force on 6 April 1993.

The benefit of private use of a car belonging to or leased by your employer is charged on a scale basis, with an additional charge if you are also provided with car fuel for private use. There is a lower charge for diesel cars.

Any contribution you make to your employer for the use of the car is deducted from the car scale charge, but there is no reduction in the car fuel charge for a contribution to the cost of fuel for private journeys. To escape the fuel charge you must reimburse the whole cost of private fuel to the employer, or pay for it yourself in the first place.

There is no tax to pay if you use a pool car made available to and used by more than one employee.

Table 12 gives details of current rates and allowances related to company cars.

TABLE 12 TABLE OF RATES AND ALLOWANCES ON CARS 1993/94

Car benefit scale rates

	Car benefit (age of car at end of year)	
Original market value up to £19,250	**Under 4 years**	**4 years or more**
	£	**£**
a) with a cylinder capacity of:		
up to 1400 cc	2,310	1,580
1401 cc to 2000 cc	2,990	2,030
2001 cc or more	4,800	3,220
b) without a cylinder capacity but original market value:		
up to £5999	2,310	1,580
£6000 to £8499	2,990	2,030
£8500 to £19,250	4,800	3,220
Original market value over £19,250		
£19,251 to £29,000	6,210	4,180
£29,001 or more	10,040	6,660

Car fuel scale rates

	Fuel benefit	
	Petrol (94/95)	**Diesel (94/95)**
	£	**£**
a) with a cylinder capacity of:		
up to 1400 cc	600 (640)	550 (580)
1401 cc to 2000 cc	760 (810)	550 (580)
2001 cc or more	1,130 (1,200)	710 (750)
b) without a cylinder capacity but original market value:		
up to £5999	600 (640)	550 (580)
£6000 to £8499	760 (810)	550 (580)
£8500 or more	1,130 (1,200)	710 (750)

Fixed profit car scheme

	First 4000 business miles	**Additional business miles**
Up to 1000 cc	26p	15p
1001cc to 1500 cc	32p	18p
1501cc to 2000 cc	40p	22p
Over 2000 cc	54p	30p

From 6 April 1994 the present system of taxing private use of cars is to be replaced by benefit charges based on the list price (or £80,000 if lower). The value will include extras supplied with the car and any accessory costing £100 or more that is added later. Cars valued at more than £15,000 and at least 15 years old at the end of the tax year will be taxed according to their open market value if this is more than the list price. Where an employee pays towards the intial cost of a car, a contribution of up to £5000 will reduce the cost on which the tax charge is based.

The taxable benefit for those who do less than 2500 business miles will be 35 per cent of the cost, reduced by a third for those who do at least 2500 but less than 18,000 business miles, and by two-thirds for those with business mileage of 18,000 miles or more. In each case, the taxable amount will be reduced by a third for cars four or more years old at the end of the tax year. Employee contributions for the use of the car will still be deducted and private fuel will still be taxed separately.

Other benefits

Table 13 illustrates the tax position regarding other benefits.

TABLE 13 SUMMARY OF MAIN BENEFIT PROVISIONS

Benefits	Tax charge	
	P11D employees	**Other employees**
Use of car	Scale charge	Not assessable
	Scale charge reduced by half if business miles are 18,000 or more	
	Scale charge is increased by half if business miles are 2500 or less, and also for second and subsequent cars	
Car fuel for private motoring	Scale charge	Cost to employer
Car parking facilities	Not assessable	Not assessable

Use of van	Fixed charge of £500 (£350 if 4 years old or more), or proportionate charge for shared vans	Not assessable
Mobile telephone	Fixed charge of £200	Not assessable
Living accommodation	Letting value (unless job related)	Letting value (unless job related)
Vouchers other than luncheon vouchers	Full value	Full value
Use of employer's credit cards	Cost of goods and services obtained	Cost of goods and services obtained
Medical insurance	Cost to employer	Not assessable
Beneficial loans (unless interest would have qualified for tax relief)	Interest at official rate less any paid, but no charge if benefit is £300	Not assessable
Loans written off	Amount written off	Amount written off
Crèche facilities	Not assessable	Not assessable
Free or subsidised canteen meals	Not assessable if available to all employees	Not assessable
Pension provision under approved schemes	Not assessable	Not assessable

Tax returns

Not everyone automatically receives a tax return each year. But if you need to declare anything then you should, especially if you are self-employed or do freelance work. If you are not sent a tax return then you should ask for one — not getting one is no excuse as the onus is on you to declare your income. The tax year runs from 6 April to 5 April the following year.

The tax return is divided into several sections which you have to fill in as necessary and if appropriate:

- income from employment, property and savings and investments for the year ended;
- deductions for the year ended;
- pensions for the year ended;
- capital gains for the year ended;
- personal tax allowances for the next year.

You should fill in your tax return within the allowed 30 days from receiving it and return it to the Inland Revenue — although there is usually no penalty for a delay of a few months. Enclose any receipts, your P60 (which is a total of the tax you have paid for the year) and any other documentation that may support your case for a tax rebate.

However, if your tax return is not returned by 31 October after the end of the tax year, you will have to pay interest from the date the tax would have been payable if the tax return had been returned on time.

Tax assessment

Sometimes before, but usually after, you send your tax return you might receive a tax assessment which shows how much tax the Inland Revenue has calculated is due, or has been overpaid. If there is a requirement to pay, you must pay this or appeal as soon as possible. If time is running out you would do best to pay the sum and argue your case later. If you do not, you could be in a lot of trouble with the Inland Revenue.

Tax-free savings

Make the most of savings that can be taken out without tax deducted. This may not pay if you are a non-taxpayer as you could probably earn more gross (without tax deducted) from alternative investments.

But for taxpayers, particularly those paying tax at 25 and 40 per cent, tax-free schemes are worth investigating. For a start, unlike savings in banks or building societies you will not be losing at least a quarter of any interest in tax.

TESSAs

TESSA is the Tax Exempt Special Savings Account. You can invest up to £9000 over five years into a TESSA from banks and building societies. The fact that tax is not deducted gives these accounts an edge.

Some schemes allow you to take interest from the account (tax free provided you do not withdraw the initial investment). The interest is paid net of tax, and the amount reserved for tax is paid as a tax-free bonus at the end of the five-year period. (See Chapter 3 for more on TESSAs.)

National Savings

You can shelter up to £24,800 over five years in National Savings Certificates and Yearly Plan. Both pay a guaranteed rate of interest. Index-linked certificates pay a set rate above inflation. (See Chapter 3 for more on National Savings.)

Ordinary account

The first £70 of annual interest is free of income tax. However, the rates are low, so it may be worth forgoing the tax saving to get a better net rate elsewhere. The minimum investment is £10 and the maximum is £10,000. Interest is paid yearly. There is no notice period.

Investment account

Interest is paid gross. However, taxpayers must then declare it. Rates are competitive.

Income bonds

Interest is paid gross. However, taxpayers must declare this income. Rates are among the highest offered by National Savings. There is a three-month notice period. The minimum investment is £2000 and the maximum £250,000. Interest is paid monthly, making it a suitable savings scheme for non-taxpayers who want a regular income from a safe investment without the hassle of reclaiming tax or registering for gross interest. Income bonds cost £1000 each and the minimum number you can buy is two.

First option bonds

First option bonds are one-year investments with interest paid yearly or on encashment. The interest rate is fixed. These bonds are aimed at basic-rate taxpayers. The minimum investment is £1000 and the maximum £250,000. Interest is paid net of tax. Non-taxpayers and reduced-rate taxpayers may reclaim tax deducted. Higher-rate taxpayers have to declare the interest and pay additional tax to bring it up to the higher rate.

Capital bonds

Capital bonds are five-year investments. Interest is paid gross but liable to tax and must be declared. They are particularly suitable for non-tax-payers who do not want income from their savings. The rate of interest is fixed. The minimum investment is £100 and the maximum £250,000 (including existing bonds). Tax must be paid each year on the interest credited, even though this interest is not paid out until the end of the five-year term.

Premium bonds

Premium bonds can hardly be viewed as savings as no interest is paid. However, prizes are paid out equal to a competitive rate of interest and prize money is tax free.

Friendly societies

You can put up to £200 a year into a 10-year tax-exempt friendly society policy. (See Chapter 3 for more on friendly society investments.)

Gilts

Gilts are free of capital gains tax.

SAYE

SAYE, or Save As You Earn, allows employees to have a regular sum deducted from their pay and put into a savings plan. You can invest up to £20 a month tax free in a Save As You Earn plan. (See Chapter 3 for more on SAYE.)

Tax-free investing

PEPs

PEPs, or Personal Equity Plans, are the tax-free way to invest in the stock market. You can shelter up to £9000 of shares, unit trusts or investment trusts each tax year in one of the these schemes. (See Chapter 3 for more on PEPs.)

Tax and your home

MIRAS

With MIRAS, or Mortgage Interest Relief At Source, on up to £30,000 of the borrowings on your main property in the UK, you get relief at the basic rate of tax (25 per cent). From 6 April 1994 tax relief will only be restricted to 20 per cent. (See Chapter 6 for more information on mortgages.)

Stamp duty

Stamp duty is normally charged on certain documents involved in transfers relating to UK property or transaction (ie share dealing). House purchases above £60,000 are charged a stamp duty of 1 per cent.

Arrange your affairs to minimise your tax

Go for gains not growth

Capital gains tax (CGT) and income tax are set at the same rate, so it may appear that there is little difference between investing in something for an income and investing for growth.

However, the advantage of going for growth is that it is much easier to avoid paying capital gains tax than income tax. For a start, fewer than 1 per cent of the population actually pays CGT. This is because you can make up to £5800 of gains on investments each tax year before having to pay tax.

The tax is on gain — not the value of the assets sold — and from 31 March 1982 includes an indexation allowance to allow for its value to rise in line with price inflation.

The other way to avoid paying CGT (other than only to make gains of less than £5800) is to 'bed and breakfast'. This financial term means that you sell an investment and buy it back immediately to realise the gain within a tax year. This stops a big capital gains tax bill building up as the tax is paid on the gain since you repurchased the investment or asset, not the original date of purchase.

Capital gains tax applies to most investments but not depreciating assets such as vintage cars and not to gilts — Government stock. There is no capital gains tax to pay on regular premium endowment policies provided you don't cash them in for 10 years.

Inheritance tax

You pay no inheritance tax as long as your estate is less than £150,000. As long as you don't die within seven years of making PETs (potentially exempt transfers), no inheritance tax is due on the yearly allowance of £3000. However, if you die within that seven-year period your inheritance tax allowances are reduced in increments.

You can also receive small sums of £250, but not in addition to the £3000. If you do not use the whole £3000 allowance in one year, you can carry it over for up to one year.

People getting married can receive one-off gifts of £5000 from each parent of the couple (over and above the £3000 annual gift), £2500 from a grandparent, and £1000 from anyone else. (See Chapter 8 regarding wills.)

Married couples

Married couples can save tax if one partner is not working or is on a lower tax rate by transferring investments into his or her name.

The higher earning partner should claim all of the married couple's allowance to get the most tax relief.

Married women can claim half the married couple's allowance as a right, but need their husband's permission to claim the full allowance. This pays where the wife is a higher-rate taxpayer and the husband a basic-rate or non-taxpayer.

But from April 1994 this tax relief will only be 20 per cent on the married couple's allowance — instead of the current 25 or 40 per cent. So rearranging your finance will no longer be worthwhile unless one partner does not have enough earnings to use up the allowance.

The other way to minimise tax between a husband and wife is if one is self-employed and the other spouse helps out with the business. By employing your partner the family can earn extra income. Up to £56 a week can be paid without national insurance or tax being incurred.

Pensions

Tax relief on pensions makes them one of the best investments. Not only do the funds grow free of tax, but you also receive tax relief at your top rate of tax. So a higher-rate taxpayer who puts £600 into a pension plan each year will get a further £400 invested by the Inland

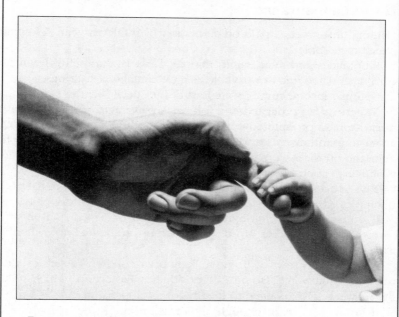

pension plan each year will get a further £400 invested by the Inland Revenue (see Chapter 8 on pensions).

National insurance

National insurance is paid on earnings which fall between set earnings bands (see Table 14).

Employees and their employers pay Class 1 contributions which are earnings related and are payable as a percentage of earnings.

National insurance funds are part of the social security system.

In general, in order to get a full basic pension, Class 1 contributions must be paid or credited equal to 52 times the lower earnings limit in at least nine in every ten years of your working life, from 16 to 65 for a man and 60 for a woman, or you must have paid 52 Class 2 or Class 3 (voluntary) contributions for those years.

You are credited with contributions when you are registered as unemployed, or unable to work because of sickness or disability.

If you are an unemployed man aged 60 or 64 you automatically receive credits whether or not you are ill or on the unemployment register.

Anyone who stays at home to look after children or sick or elderly relatives usually has Home Responsibilities Protection, which reduces the number of years need to qualify for a full pension.

If you do not earn enough, either as an employee or in your self-employment, to pay enough Class 1 or 2 contributions, you can pay voluntary Class 3 contributions to help qualify for the retirement and widow's pension.

Late contributions can be paid for the previous six years.

Reduced rate for certain married women and widows

Women who were married or widowed as at 6 April 1977 may have chosen on or before 11 May 1977 to pay Class 1 contributions at a reduced rate. If they are still entitled to pay the reduced contributions, they hold certificate CF 383 which must be handed over to the employer to enable contributions to be deducted at the correct time.

If a married women is self-employed, the election makes her exempt from paying Class 2 contributions, but not Class 4 contributions.

A wife who pays a reduced-rate contribution is not eligible to receive contributory benefits, such as her own pension, but she can claim a retirement and widow's pension on the contribution record of her husband. She is also entitled to receive statutory sick pay and statutory maternity pay.

Warning

It is possible to backdate contributions to qualify for a full pension, but it may not be worthwhile if the woman will qualify for a reduced (60 per cent) pension based on her husband's contributions. However, divorcees and widows should check with the contributions agency to see if backdating is worthwhile.

People over pensionable age

No contributions are payable by an employee who is over pension age (65 for men, 60 for women).

More than one employment

Where a person has more than one employment, he or she is liable to pay primary Class 1 contributions for each job. There is, however, a prescribed annual maximum contribution.

The maximum is based on 53 weeks. The amounts for 1993/94 are:

All employments not contracted out	All employments contracted out	Reduced rate
£1795.64	£1448.49	£857.01

TABLE 14 NATIONAL INSURANCE CONTRIBUTION RATES

	6/4/93–5/4/94	1994/95
Lower earnings limit per week (LEL)	£56	£57
Upper earnings limit per week (UEL)	£420	£430

Employees pay no contributions if their weekly earnings are below the lower earnings limit.

Otherwise they are liable as below:
Not contracted out

	6/4/93–5/4/94	1994/95
– earnings up to LEL	2.0%	2.0%
– balance of earnings up to UEL	9.0%	10.0%

Reduced rate for certain married women and widows
% payable on all earnings to UEL

	6/4/93–5/4/94	1994/95
providing earnings exceed LEL	3.85%	3.85%

	6/4/93–5/4/94	1994/95
Self-employed		
Class 2 contributions per week	£5.55	£5.65
Class 4 contributions rate	6.3%	7.3%
on profits between	£6340 & £21,840	£6490 & £22,360

Non-taxpayers

Tax saving tips

If you are a non-taxpayer you do not have to pay tax on your savings.

Yet millions are doing just that. Some 15 million non-taxpayers can register to receive interest on their banks and building society savings tax free.

These include pensioners, married women and children. The reason why many are still paying tax is because they do not know it is automatically deducted. Since 6 April 1991, however, non-taxpayers have been able to register to have their interest paid with no tax deducted.

How to register

Get Inland Revenue leaflet IR110 from your bank, building society or local tax office. It includes the registration form R85 which you then send to your bank or building society. You need a separate form for each account you have.

You can also reclaim tax already deducted over the previous 12 months. Leaflets IR111 and IR112 give full details.

The Inland Revenue Freephone service 0800 660800 can also give advice.

On a joint account, non-taxpayers can claim back tax deducted on their share of the interest.

The same rules apply to share dividends. These automatically have tax deducted, but non-taxpayers can claim this back.

Those who pay tax at the 20 per cent rate can claim the difference between the 25 per cent deducted from savings interest and the 20 per cent they pay.

However, share dividends are taxed at a different rate. For dividends paid after 5 April 1993, the tax credit is 20 per cent. Dividends are paid with tax deducted. However, those who pay tax at the 25 per cent rate do not have to pay any additional tax. However, 40 per cent tax payers have to pay extra tax on the difference between the 40 per cent rate and the 20 per cent credited. Therefore, a net dividend of £75 comes with a tax credit of £93.75 (93.75 – 20% = £75) and a higher rate tax payer will be left with £56.25 (93.75 – 40% = £56.25).

Tax and the family

- *Share your investments* Married couples can save tax if one partner is not working or is on a lower tax rate by transferring investments into his or her name.
- *Married at last* Tell your tax office when you get married and they will give you an extra married couple's allowance of £1720 a year.
- *Married couple's allowance* In this tax year, the higher-earning partner should claim the married couple's allowance to get the most tax relief. But from April 1994 you will only get tax relief at 20 per cent on the married couple's allowance.
- *Career wives* Married women can claim half the allowance as a right. If the wife is the higher earner or the husband is not working, he can agree to transfer the full alowance to her to save tax.
- *Employ your partner* If you are self-employed and your spouse gives you unpaid help, you could pay him or her up to £56 a week and not be liable for any tax or national insurance.

£ **Tax tips** £

- Let out a room. If you take a lodger for under £271 a month, you won't have to pay tax on the income.
- If you have not got a pension, think about starting one because you get tax relief at your highest rate on contributions.
- Make up for lost time. You can make extra contributions to a personal pension and benefit from unused tax relief from the past seven years.
- If you are over 65 make sure you get your higher personal allowance of £4200 and the higher married couple's allowance of £2465. For those over 75 the allowances rise to £4370 and £2505.
- Keep your income down. If your total income is more than £14,200 your age-related allowances are cut by £1 for every £2 you exceed the limit. So keep taxable income down with tax-free investments like TESSAs or PEPs.
- Make a will. It could save on inheritance tax.
- Be generous. Gifts of up to £3000 each tax year are free from inheritance tax.

- Wedding presents. Parents can give up to £5000 tax free to a child when he or she marries. Grandparents can give £2500 and other wellwishers up to £1000.
- Health insurance. Over-60s get tax relief on private medical insurance policies. But policies that offer a cash benefit are not eligible.
- Ask if you can take part of your earnings under a profit-related pay scheme. It is tax free up to either one-fifth of your pay or £4000, whichever is the lower.
- Sign up for share options. There is no tax to pay on shares from an approved Save As You Earn share option scheme.
- Bright sparks. Payments of up to £5000 for staff suggestions are tax free.
- Cash or car? The tax treatment of company cars is making them less attractive as a perk. Consider asking your employer for cash instead.
- Use a pool car. There is no tax to pay if you use a pool car made available to and used by more than one employee.
- Bump up your business miles. If you do more than 18,000 business miles a year in your company car, the scale charge is halved. If you do fewer than 2,500 miles it is increased by 50 per cent.

8

Planning for and making the most of retirement

You may have to live for 20 years or more on the savings, investments and pension you build up during your working life.

Even if you manage to work for a full 40 years without interruption, it means you could have six months of retirement for every year you are earning.

It does not take a genius to work out that it will take a lot of planning to maintain your lifestyle when you retire.

These are the golden rules to remember when planning for your retirement:

- Do not rely on the basic state pension — it will not provide you with a reasonable standard of living and many people don't even get the full amount because they haven't paid in 44 years' national insurance contributions (39 years for women) needed to qualify.
- Do not assume you will automatically get the state pension — not everyone qualifies.
- Men under 40 and women under 35 who are not contracted out of the State Earnings Related Pension Scheme (SERPS) with a company pension scheme should consider contracting out with a personal pension. Over 30s are given a 1 per cent incentive by the Government to contract out.
- If you haven't got a pension plan, sign up for one as soon as you can. The self-employed and those not eligible for a company scheme can take out a personal pension from an insurance company.
- Do not delay saving for your retirement — the earlier you start the cheaper it will be and the higher the pension you will be able to afford.
- Make the most of tax relief — basic-rate taxpayers get 25p from the

Inland Revenue for every 75p they invest and higher-rate taxpayers 40p for every 60p.

- Try to pay in the maximum allowed. For members of employers' schemes, that is 15 per cent of earnings. The limit for personal pensions starts at 17.5 per cent of earnings for those aged 35 and under and rises to 40 per cent for those over 60.
- Contribute as much as you can. Even if you build up a nest egg of £100,000, this will only provide you with an income of around £5000 to £8000 on retirement.
- Make up for lost time. You can boost your employer's pension by making additional voluntary contributions (AVCs) or free-standing AVCs to an insurance company, using up to 15 per cent of your earnings.
- Personal pension plan holders can backdate contributions for up to six years to make use of unused tax relief.

Basic state pension

If you are planning to live off the state pension alone in retirement, think again. The full rate is just £56.10 a week for a single person in the 1993–94 tax year which runs to 5 April 1994. In 1994–95 it is due to rise to £57.60.

Married couples can qualify for a higher pension of £89.80 a week, based on the husband's pension entitlement (£92.10 from 1994/95). If both husband and wife qualify for the full basic pension, they can receive £112.20 a week (£115.20 from 1994/95).

The basic pension rises each April in line with the Retail Price Index up to the previous September.

Will I qualify for a basic state pension?

Contrary to popular belief you are not automatically entitled to the basic state pension. Check what you are entitled to before undertaking any other pension planning.

You qualify for the basic state pension if you pay in enough national insurance (NI) contributions. How much pension you will receive depends on how many 'qualifying years' you have built up — these are tax years which run from April to April in which you have paid enough NI contributions. It is possible to pay some NI during a year but not enough for that year to count towards your pension. If at least

90 per cent of the years in your working life are qualifying years, you should get the full basic pension.

Nearly everyone who works has Class 1 contributions automatically deducted from their pay (for rates of contributions see Chapter 7). These count towards the basic state pension.

However, if you earn less than a certain amount you do not pay national insurance or build up any pension credits. This is known as the lower earnings limit and is set at £56 a week for the 1993–94 tax year (£57 for 1994/95).

Some married women who have opted to pay a special low rate of national insurance are not building up a basic pension either.

The self-employed build up their pension entitlement by paying a different type of national insurance contribution known as Class 2.

Those registered as unemployed or claiming certain state benefit such as unemployment, maternity or sickness benefit are usually credited with national insurance, as are men within five years of state pension age who are unemployed, who are credited without the need to 'sign on' as unemployed.

Those who stay at home to care for children or relatives may qualify for Home Responsibilities Protection which reduces the length of the national insurance record you need in order to qualify for a basic pension.

How much national insurance makes a qualifying year?

Employees who pay Class 1 national insurance contributions must pay national insurance on earnings equal to, or more than the weekly lower earnings limit which is £56 for the 1993–94 tax year and £57 for the 1994–95 year. Reduced contributions paid by some married women do not count.

The self-employed must make 52 Class 2 payments (Class 4 contributions do not count). These are a flat rate of £5.55 a week in 1993–94 and £5.65 in the 1994–95 tax year.

Alternatively 52 payments of Class 3 contributions which are paid at a flat rate of £5.45 each week in the 1993–94 tax year and £5.55 in 1994–95 can be paid. A mix of these options can be paid.

How do I find out how much pension I will get?

If you fit into one of the above categories or have gaps in your national insurance payment record, you should request a pensions forecast from the Retirement Pensions Forecast and Advisory (RPFA) Service.

This will tell you if you qualify for a pension, explain how much state pension you have built up so far and give details of your expected pension at retirement. It will also tell you what you can do to increase your entitlement.

ACTION

You are allowed to have up to one forecast a year. To use the service, get Form BR19 from any DSS office, complete it and send it to the address given on the form.

Table 15 describes how the basic state pension is calculated.

TABLE 15 HOW THE REDUCED BASIC STATE PENSION IS CALCULATED

Number of qualifying years	Percentage of full pension given	
	Women	Men
9 or less	0	0
10	26	0
11	29	25
12	31	28
13	34	30
14	36	32
15	39	35
16	42	37
17	44	39
18	47	41
19	49	44
20	52	46
21	54	48
22	57	50
23	59	53
24	62	55
25	65	57
26	67	60
27	70	62
28	72	64
29	75	66
30	77	69

Number of qualifying years	Percentage of full pension given	
	Women	Men
31	80	71
32	83	73
33	85	75
34	88	78
35	90	80
36	93	82
37	95	85
38	98	87
39	100	89
40	100	91
41	100	94
42	100	96
43	100	98
44 or more	100	100

Qualifying years are those in which you have paid sufficient national insurance contributions. If at least 90 per cent of the years in your working life are qualifying years, you should get the full basic pension.

Your working life begins on 6 April of the tax year in which you reach 16 and ends on 5 April of the tax year in which you reach 64 (men) or 59 (women) if you were born after 5 July 1932. (This will change when pension ages are equalised at 65 for men and women from 2020).

Those born before 5 July 1932 have a working life calculated on whether or not they were in the old state pension scheme on 5 July 1948. If they were not contributing to that scheme, their working life begins on 6 April 1948. If they were, it begins on 6 April for the tax year before 1948 in which they last started to contribute to the scheme.

Can I pay extra to ensure I get the basic state pension or to increase the pension I will get?

Yes. If you are not entitled to the full basic state pension or any pension at all, you can pay in extra national insurance contributions.

Class 3 national insurance contributions, which are set at £5.45 for the 1993–94 tax year (rising to £5.55 from April 1994), can be paid to fill gaps in your payment record. However, you can only backdate this for six years. And if you paid the married women's reduced rate you cannot then make up for this shortfall by making Class 3 contributions.

When do I get the basic state pension?

If you retire early you will not get the basic state pension, which is only paid to men when they reach 65 and to women when they reach 60. However, women whose pension is based on their husband's pension must wait until the husband reaches 65. These state retirement ages are currently under review and women will retire from age 65 from the year 2020. No woman over the age of 43 will be affected. The new retirement age will be phased in from 2010.

If you want to continue to work, you can put off starting to receive the state pension for up to five years. In return your pension will be boosted by 7.5 per cent for each year you delay retirement. Or you can continue to work and receive your full pension at the same time.

State Earnings Related Pension Scheme (SERPS)

SERPS is a top-up to the basic state pension which is built up by employees. It is earnings related, which means the more you earn the more you get, and like the basic state pension is built up from your national insurance contributions.

Not all earnings are taken into account — only those on which you pay full-rate national insurance contributions.

The pension is based on an average of these earnings over your whole working life for those retiring from 6 April 1999 onwards. Those retiring before then have SERPS pension based on their best 20 years' earnings (or as many years' earnings as they have built up since 1978). The maximum you will get if you are a member of SERPS for as many years as possible is £4022 for those retiring in 1995–96, rising to £4681 for those who reach state pension age in the tax year 2000–01 (based on 1993–94 earnings limits).

However, SERPS pensions will be reduced if you have worked for less than the maximum number of years or earned less than the upper earnings limit for national insurance (which is £420 a week for the 1993–94 tax year).

Some people are deemed to have zero earnings for SERPS. These include the self-employed, those earning so little they do not pay national insurance (the lower earnings limit for NI in 1993–94 tax year is £56 per week), married women paying reduced rate NI, the unemployed and those paying Class 3 NI.

SERPS is paid when you reach state retirement age and as with the basic state pension your SERPS pension will be increased by 7.5 per cent for each year you defer taking your pension (up to a maximum of five years).

After retirement SERPS pensions are increased each year in line with changes in the Retail Price Index.

There is also an old state earnings-related pension which ran from 6 April 1961 to 5 April 1975.

As with the basic state pension you can get a statement of your current SERPS entitlement and a forecast of what it could be by retirement. Get Form BR19 from DSS offices.

Roughly half Britain's employed workforce are paying a lower rate of national insurance and not building up a right to a pension from SERPs. Instead their company pension guarantees them a pension equivalent to SERPs — this is known as 'contracting out'.

Of the other half, less than 10 million employees who are not in a company pension scheme, about five million have also contracted out of SERPS and have some of their and their employer's NI contributions paid into a personal pension.

Employees who are already in contracted-out company pension schemes, and those in superannuation schemes such as those run for civil servants and teachers, cannot contract out with a personal pension.

Contracting out of SERPS

The ageing population means that the costs of providing SERPS have soared. As a result the Government encourages members who are not contracted out via their company pension scheme to opt out, known as contracting out. The NI rebates must be paid into a personal pension plan.

Incentives have been offered to those who contract out and at the same time SERPS pensions will be reduced for those who stay in the scheme.

How do I know if I am in SERPS?

If you are an employee paying full-rate national insurance contributions (£56 or more a week in the 1993–94 tax year) you are eligible for SERPS. The self-employed are not members of SERPS.

How do I know if I am already contracted out?

If you are a member of an employer scheme you are probably already contracted out of SERPS (check with your company pension scheme trustees).

If you are contracting out through a final pay scheme this will give you an entitlement to a guaranteed minimum pension (GMP) which ensures that you cannot lose by contracting out through a final pay scheme.

If you are in a contracted-out money purchase scheme (COMP), the employer's scheme does not guarantee the amount of pension you will receive to replace SERPS. Instead your employer must pay in a set amount equivalent to the amount that you and your employer have saved by paying lower national insurance contributions.

If you contract out, the scheme or plan provider must increase the pension at a rate of 3 per cent a year or by the rate of inflation if this is less. This ruling applies to GMPs built up since 6 April 1988 and affects personal penions built up from 1 July 1988 onwards.

How much will I get if I contract out of SERPS?

This depends on how much you earn between the lower earnings limit for national insurance (£56 a week in 1993–94; £57 for 1994–95) and the upper earnings limit after which no national insurance is paid (£420 a week for 1993–94; £430 for 1994–95).

Rebates have been reduced. The rebate was set at 5.8 per cent of earnings between the two earnings limits for the five years from April 1988 to April 1993. Of this, 2 per cent represented a rebate of the national insurance you paid and 3.8 per cent represented a rebate of the national insurance paid on your behalf by your employer.

If you had not already been contracted out of SERPS you also qualified for a special incentive bonus which was equal to a further 2 per cent of your earnings between the two bands. Also tax relief on the employee's share of the rebate meant the total was 8.48 per cent.

As from 6 April 1993 these rates have been cut to 4.8 per cent. The revised rate will apply until 5 April 1996. Of this, 1.8 per cent represents a rebate of your national insurance and 3 per cent that of your employer. Tax relief on employee's share pushes the total to 5.4 per cent.

In addition, there is a 1 per cent incentive payable to everyone aged 30 or over who is contracted out through a personal pension plan. This is no longer linked to being newly contracted out, but is only available to those who contract out through a personal pension plan.

In addition tax relief is given at the basic rate on the 1.8 per cent of earnings that represent your own national insurance contributions. This represents another 0.6 per cent of your earnings betwen the upper and lower earnings limits. This brings the total rebate for those over 30 to 6.4 per cent of relevant earnings (£420 – £56 = £364) or a maximum of £23.30 a week (£1211 a year).

How to work out a SERPS rebate to a personal pension

1. Calculate your weekly pay.
2. Deduct the lower earnings limit (£56 for 1993–94)
3. If the remainder is above £364 use this for the calculations; if not use the figure as calculated in step 2.
4. If you are under 30 work out 5.4 per cent of the above figure. If you are over 30 work out 6.4 per cent. If you are in a COMP scheme run by your employer the calculation is based on 4.8 per cent.
5. Multiply by 52 to give the annual rebate.
   NB The bands change to £57 and £430 from April 1994.

Example:

If you earn £256 a week, deduct the lower earnings limit £56 = £200.

Then work out the relevant percentage. So if you qualify for a 5.4 per cent rebate this will be £200/100 × 5.4 = £10.80.

Multiply this by 52 to give the annual rebate: £10.80 × 52 = £561.60.

Who will benefit from contracting out?

This depends on your sex, age, view of future investment performance, your earnings and the size of the rebate and any incentive payments you may receive.

SERPS pensions are being cut back for people retiring after the end of this century. The cutbacks are being phased in gradually, so the earlier you reach state pension age the more SERPS pension you would give up through contracting out. This is because the rebates you receive are at a flat rate — they do not take account of how much you have already earned in SERPS.

As the rebates are the same regardless of age, younger workers who have built up little SERPS entitlement are better off contracting out. This is the case if you earn more than £9500 a year when contracting out first time and £7500 a year if you have already contracted out. This ensures rebates are large enough to cover insurance companies' charges on personal pensions.

As a general rule, males up to 40 and women up to 35 are better off contracting out. But the exact age will vary from person to person. After these ages it is generally better to stay in SERPS — and if you have already contracted out you may be better off contracting back in again.

What if my circumstances change?

As you get older you should review whether to remain contracted out, as after a certain age you will be better off contracting back in.

If you lose your job or earn less than the minimum on which full-rate national insurance is paid, you will not get any SERPS rebates for that period as you have not built up any entitlement.

If you move jobs and want to join the company's pension scheme, check whether it is contracted out or not. If it is contracted out and you want to join the scheme to take advantage of your employer's contributions, you must put your personal pension on hold. What is invested will continue to grow but no further pension contributions will be made either from you or from SERPS rebates.

How do I go about it?

All SERPS rebates must be paid into a personal pension. You cannot take the money now. So to contract out of SERPS you must go to a personal pension plan provider. These are mainly life insurance companies. Personal pensions are sold by life insurance companies, banks, building societies and a range of financial advisers (see Chapter 9 for where to get advice).

If you are in an employer pension scheme that is not contracted out you can take out a personal pension plan to get your SERPS rebates. This can either be a rebate-only personal pension plan or a freestanding Additional Voluntary Contribution scheme. However, as you are not allowed to pay into a company pension and a personal pension at the same time (unless you have income from various sources) you cannot pay any of your own contributions into the personal pension.

Company pension schemes

Over 10 million employees are members of pension schemes run by their employers. In addition to a pension these schemes often include extra benefits such as life insurance and pensions for widows and children.

Most involve the employer paying in contributions as well as the employee.

Part of the proceeds can usually be taken as a tax-free lump sum at retirement.

Schemes may be open to all employees or restricted to just those in a particular group. You do not have to join the scheme and if you are already a member you can leave the scheme.

How much pension you build up depends on the type of scheme.

Final salary schemes

These pay out a pension based on your salary at, or near, retirement and the number of years that you have been in the scheme. You usually get either one-eightieth or one-sixtieth of your pre-retirement pay for each year in the scheme.

The advantage of these schemes is that your pension will keep pace with your earnings and you will get a set, known as defined, benefit. However, these schemes can penalise job changers.

Final salary is usually defined as your earnings in any one year out of the last five years before retirement, or the yearly average of your earnings during a three-year period ending any time within the last ten years before retirement. If you have not worked for the full 40 years to build up a maximum pension you can build up a maximum pension over a shorter period. Ask your scheme trustees.

Money purchase schemes

These pay out a pension based on what you and your employer have paid into the scheme. Unlike final salary schemes your pension is not set. It will depend on how much you put in, how well your money is invested and what that investment will 'buy' in terms of a pension when you retire.

These schemes are better for those who change jobs frequently, as unlike final salary schemes the pension is based on what is paid in not how long you have worked for the same employer.

Some employers run schemes that are a combination of both final salary and money purchase schemes. There are also the following types of scheme: average pay schemes, based on pay throughout your working life; salary grade schemes, where employees earn a set amount of pension based on salary bands; and flat-rate schemes, which give a set rate of pension for each year you are in the scheme.

How much can I pay in?

Pensions benefit from significant tax advantages so the Inland Revenue puts some limits on the amount you can pay in and the maximum you can take out.

The amount you can contribute if you are in an employer's scheme is limited to 15 per cent of earnings. The total you contribute to the employer's scheme and as additional voluntary contributions cannot exceed this maximum.

If you belong to a scheme set up on or after 14 March 1989, or which you joined after 1 June 1989, there is also a limit on the amount of cash you can contribute. The limit for the 1993–94 tax year is £11,250.

TABLE 16 THE MOST YOU CAN PAY INTO A PENSION

Yearly earnings	Maximum yearly contributions	Cost after tax relief
£10,000	£1,500	£1,125 (25% tax relief)
£15,000	£2,250	£1,688 (25% tax relief)
£20,000	£3,000	£2,250 (25% tax relief)
£25,000	£3,750	£2,813 (25% tax relief)
£25,000	£3,750	£2,250 (40% tax relief)
£30,000	£4,500	£2,700 (40% tax relief)
£40,000	£6,000	£3,600 (40% tax relief)
£50,000	£7,500	£4,500 (40% tax relief)

For *final pay schemes* the restriction is on the pension you can take on retirement. This is restricted to £50,000 for the 1993–94 tax year for schemes set up on or after 14 March 1989 or which were joined on after 1 June 1989 (51,200 for 1994–95).

The lump sum is restricted to one and a half times final pay up to a maximum of £112,500 (in the 1993–94 tax year; 115,200 for 1994–95).

Some schemes provide a cash lump sum at retirement as well as a pension. With other schemes you can choose to swap part of your pension for a lump sum.

However, this will reduce the amount of pension you receive. There are limits, set by the Inland Revenue, on how much of your pension you can take as a cash sum.

When can I take my pension?

Employer pension schemes can start paying out a pension even if you have not reached state retirement age. Depending on when the scheme was set up or when you joined, this can either be from age 50 or from 60 for men and 55 for women.

Certain professions which have a short career life, such as divers or professional footballers, can retire earlier with a full pension. However, if you retire early your pension will be reduced — often by a significant amount. If you retire early due to ill health, you are likely to get a better deal. Increasingly schemes are requiring that both men and women retire at age 65.

How much do I pay?

This varies with the scheme. Some are non-contributory which means that the employer pays the whole cost. Most involve payments by the employee and these are known as contributory. Contributions are usually around 5 per cent of salary with your employer paying a further amount of salary. In final salary, the employer's amount is not specified.

But with final salary schemes the employer will provide however much is needed to make up the balance of the cost of providing the pension and other benefits. Both you and your employer get tax relief on contributions to an employer scheme. If your scheme is in surplus (it has an excess of funds) your employer can take a contribution holiday.

What happens when I retire?

You will usually be given a choice of whether you want to take the whole of your retirement fund as a pension or whether you want to take part of it as a lump sum.

Your pension from a money purchase scheme is bought using an annuity. These are bought at retirement and provide an income for life. If you have a lump sum from your pension scheme you can invest in one of these. If you have invested in a personal pension plan you must use the final payout to buy an annuity. You can shop around to get a better deal.

Once you have bought an annuity you cannot get your money back, so you must weigh up a number of factors before taking one out. If you are in poor health you may not live long enough to get a good return from your annuity. On the other hand, if longevity runs in your family, an annuity may be a good bet.

Annuity rates — how much income you get from your lump sum — are based on, among other things, how long you are likely to live.

As a rough guide you should expect an income of around £8000 on a £100,000 lump sum. So if you pass away after two years you would only have got £16,000 back.

But part of each annuity payment is treated as the return of your original investment and is tax free. The remaining income is taxable.

You can buy an annuity that provides a flat-rate pension for life, one that pays a rising rate of income either in line with inflation or another set percentage rate or a joint annuity with your spouse.

What about inflation eating into my pension?

You can buy an annuity that protects you against inflation.

The largest pension schemes tend to offer a guaranteed increase up to a limited level of, say, 5 per cent. Discretionary increases can also be made.

What if I want to boost my pension?

You can make extra contributions to boost your company pension as long as your total contributions remain within the tax limits. Your extra payments are called Additional Voluntary Contributions (AVCs).

You can either have an AVC linked to your employer's scheme or your own free-standing AVC, which is a scheme independent of your employer's pension arrangements usually run by a life insurance company. Most are money purchase but some employers with final salary schemes have AVC schemes which allow you to 'buy' extra years in the scheme (not that common these days).

How do I know that my company pension is safe?

Despite the publicity surrounding the Maxwell scandal in which money was plundered from Mirror pension schemes, most company pension schemes are very safe.

However, you do have certain rights to check up on your pension scheme. This is the information you are entitled to from your company pension scheme trustees:

- *Annual statement of benefits* This will tell you what your estimated total pension will be when you retire and what it would be if you took a lump sum. It also details any death benefits and any pensions to be given to your spouse or dependants, plus details of the scheme finances.
- *Type of scheme.*
- *Membership* Who is eligible, what conditions apply to membership, whether membership is automatic or not, period of notice for opting out (if any).
- *Contributions* How they are calculated.
- *Benefits* Normal pension age under the scheme, benefits payable, how they are calculated and conditions for payment, discretionary benefits, whether benefits are funded or not, whether there is any provision to increase pensions in payment, early leaver benefits.
- *Trustees* Who they are and the address to which enquiries about the scheme should be sent.

Executive schemes and small self-administered schemes have their own special arrangements and are designed either for managers or those running small firms.

Personal pensions

Personal pensions are a way of making your own pension provision if you are not a member of an employer's scheme.

Few people want to think about retirement in their 20s or 30s, but that is exactly when it pays to start investing in a personal pension. The decision of whether or not to plan for retirement is often made for those in company pension schemes as they tend to join automatically.

But those without a company scheme have to make a consious decision to take out a personal pension. They must decide how much they are prepared to pay in and who will manage their scheme for them.

The earlier one of these schemes is taken out the better. A five-year delay for a man aged 30 could mean 40 per cent less income when it comes to retirement.

Thanks to the Government's incentives and national insurance rebates for those who contract out of SERPS, these personal pensions do not have to cost a penny. However, it is vital to make some of your own contributions.

Anyone who is at least 16 and under the age of 75 with earnings can take out a personal pension plan. But you cannot belong to an employer's pension scheme and pay into a personal pension plan at the same time unless:

- you have additional earnings from another source other than the employer;
- the personal pension plan is used solely for 'contracting out';
- you are taxed on contributions made by your employer to the scheme on your behalf; but the majority of ordinary employees will not have an unapproved scheme (FURB) available.

How much can I pay in?

The limits on contributions are set by the Inland Revenue and rise with age. The percentage limits only apply on earnings up to £75,000 (£76,800 from April 1994). The limit usually rises in line with inflation each year, but there have been exceptions when it has been left unchanged. Table 17 gives details of current contribution limits.

TABLE 17 PERSONAL PENSION CONTRIBUTION LIMITS

Age on 6 April	% of pay	Maximum contribution
35 or less	17.5	£13,125
36–45	20.0	£15,000
46–50	25.0	£18,750
51–55	30.0	£22,500
56–60	35.0	£26,250
61 or over	40.0	£30,000
Life assurance (out of above)	5.0	£3,750

Maximum net relevant earnings of £75,000 relate to pay for the employed and earnings minus any business expenses for the self-employed.

The minimum that can generally be paid into a personal pension plan is £30 a month or £1000 as a one-off lump-sum payment.

How do I choose a personal pension?

Investment performance must come top of your list of priorities. It is difficult to compare how well a life insurance company's fund managers will do in the future.

All life insurance companies must quote standard investment projections which were set at 13 per cent and 8.5 per cent, but have recently been reduced to 10.5 per cent and 6 per cent. Remember, there is no guarantee that these figures will be achieved, they are only an illustration.

Past performance can be compared. Pick a company that is a consistently good performer. Magazines like *Money Management* and *Planned Savings* are available in many libraries and newsagents and list past performance. Alternatively, ask your financial adviser where the life company ranks in performance tables.

What kind of personal pension should I pick?

There are basically two types of personal pension: with-profits and unit-linked, plus a newer version of with-profits policies called unitised with-profits:

- *With-profits* contracts are designed to iron out fluctuations in investment performance. Each year an annual or reversionary bonus is added to your policy. This is your share of the investment growth of the pension fund for that year. Once added these bonuses cannot be taken away, but the level of bonus can vary from year to year.

  At the end of the policy term, a final or terminal bonus is added. This is not guaranteed and can be increased or cut.

  With-profits policies are not that common these days.

- *Unit-linked* pensions are slightly more volatile in that they are directly linked to the underlying value of the investment fund. You build up units in this fund. The drawback of these funds is if the stockmarket crashes just before you retire your pension will be reduced. But usually there will be a 'safer' fund which you can switch into as you approach retirement and need to consolidate gains made.

- *Unitised with-profits* pensions are a simpler version of with-profits contracts.

When can I take my pension?

Personal pensions can be taken from age 50 to 75. Old-style pre-1988 personal pensions, known as Section 226 (now known as Section 620) contracts, can only be taken from 60 onwards.

What if I die before I reach retirement?

With most personal pensions taken out since 1988, the pension fund you have built up will be paid to your estate or nominated beneficiaries. Some older pension contracts only repay your contributions. Check with your plan provider.

Is it worth taking out life cover with my personal pension?

Yes. This is a very tax efficient way of buying term assurance — life cover that protects you during the term of the contract but does not give you a lump sum at the end. However, if you stop your contributions you must remember that you no longer have cover.

9

Where to get help and advice and how to complain effectively

How to be your own financial adviser

The best person to plan your finances is ... you. You are the only person you can really trust to make sure that mistakes are not made or that you are not duped in any way. You have to have ultimate responsibility for all the financial decisions that you have to make.

Even when you seek financial advice you should still remember that you are ultimately responsible for your own finances. It is a case of buyer beware.

If you want to make your own investment decisions you will need to be as well informed as a financial adviser. This is not easy. While performance charts are published in newspapers and financial magazines, this will only tell you about a particular company's performance in terms of investment. You will also need to know how good its administration is, how its charges compare and how financially sound the company is. That is why it is recommended that you seek professional advice when making long-term financial decisions.

How to pick a financial adviser

Before approaching any financial adviser (otherwise known as an insurance broker or intermediary) you should have a fair idea of what you can afford to spend and what your needs are. That way you will not be swayed into parting with more than you want or investing in something that does not really meet your long-term financial goals.

The adviser is there to advise you on the amounts you need to spend on an investment or insurance or pension plan to get the best returns and which products offer the best deals.

FEES VERSUS COMMISSION?

Boyton Financial Services Limited (BFS) is one of the few firms of independent advisers that <u>only</u> operates on a time-spent fee charging basis. All discounts and commissions are rebated directly back to you, the client.

We have developed a highly refined and comprehensive financial planning service, on a fee and retainer basis. Appropriate to investors at all levels, it can provide worthwhile savings.

BFS also operates an *execution only service* for a flat fee of £105, for the more sophisticated investor who merely wishes their decisions to be implemented.

For further information on our range of services and fee structure call or write to: Boyton Financial Services Limited, PO Box 14, Halstead, Essex CO9 4DY. Telephone: 0787 61919.

DAVIS DRUCKMAN
FINANCIAL SERVICES LTD
Albany House
324/326 Regent Street, London W1R 5AA
Telephone: 071 255 2330

We are **Independent Financial Advisers** and are **NOT** tied to any individual Insurance Company. We offer a comprehensive and individual service embracing both corporate and personal insurance and mortgage matters.

OUR SERVICES INCLUDE:
- PENSIONS
- LIFE INSURANCE
- INVESTMENT BONDS
- MORTGAGES
- PERSONAL EQUITY PLANS

Call us now for a no obligation discussion on
071 255 2330

THE PRINCIPLES UNDERLYING OUR CLIENT RELATIONSHIP

Integrity
We will observe high standards of integrity and fair dealing.

Skill
We will act with due skill, care and diligence, and will always provide the highest quality service.

Information about Clients
We will always obtain from our clients the information which might reasonably be expected to be relevant in giving independent advice.

Information for Clients
We will always take reasonable steps to give to our clients, in a comprehensive and timely manner, any information needed to enable him or her to make a balanced and informed decision.

You can go to a tied agent, a high street insurance broker, a bank, building society, financial adviser or to a salesman who works for just one company.

Financial advisers are split into two sorts — independent advisers who can recommend the products of all companies and those that are tied or linked to just one company, who will offer you the most suitable product but only from the selection of products offered by the firm they are tied to.

Always check that the investment firm and adviser you deal with are authorised. Under the Financial Services Act anyone giving financial advice to the public must be authorised and regulated by one of the financial watchdogs. If they are not then they are breaking the law.

To check that the firm you have approached or been approached by is authorised, ask them which watchdog they are registered with and then check them out. Alternatively, you can ring the Securities and Investments Board (SIB) and check the firm and their SIB number against SIB's central register (tel: 071-638 1240). Don't go ahead and sign *anything* until you have done this simple task.

Most of the independent intermediaries will be registered with a self regulatory organisation, FIMBRA. Banks and building societies tend to be tied to life insurance companies, with a few exceptions, and will be regulated by LAUTRO, as will company representatives and tied agents of life insurance companies.

LAUTRO and FIMBRA are due to merge to become the PIA — the Personal Investment Authority. IMRO — the investment managers organisation — may be the regulator for fund management companies. Other advisers can be regulated by professional bodies.

All financial advisers are bound by the Financial Services Act to give you 'suitable advice'. In the case of independent financial advisers, this means they must give good advice on a wide range of financial products from various source companies.

The result is that the adviser has to recommend the most appropriate products to suit your financial needs and circumstances. In order to find out just what your needs are, you will have to provide the adviser with enough information so that the 'know your customer' rules can be met. The adviser is not allowed by law to recommend products just because they pay the best commission.

Do you really want to pay less tax?

Why ...

- are you leaving money in a building society deposit account?
- are you holding shares/unit trusts directly instead of via a PEP?
- do you make payments to an endowment savings plan but not to a friendly society?
- aren't you using your annual capital gains tax exemption?

Forward planning and separate taxation are just two of the many strategies that can be used to reduce or mitigate tax.

Last year £1.2 billion was paid in inheritance tax alone, but it wasn't the super rich who paid this tax, it was ordinary people some of whom hadn't even made a will!

In total an estimated £8 billion was wasted in the tax year 92/93 by people paying tax unnecessarily. Are you one of them?

Do you really want to retire early?

Are you making full use of your pension allowances? You cannot carry tax relief over into later tax years on additional voluntary pension contributions — are you losing this benefit?

Self-employed and profitable? You have the huge advantage of being able to claim back tax paid in previous years and saving your current taxable profits for your own future use. Would you like to do this?

Of the 11 million employees in occupational pension schemes, 3 million have no chance of retiring on a full two-thirds of final salary.

I realise that this brief article will not apply to 'most people'. If what they tell me is true, 'most people' are going to live forever, never be ill or injured and retire early on full pay. So if you are not like 'most people' and would like to plan your future, please be sure to speak to an experienced independent adviser who covers all aspects of financial planning and who is FIMBRA registered.

Rod Murdison

Rod Murdison joined the financial services industry in June 1981. He is an appointed representative of the Financial Options Network — a group of FIMBRA registered independent financial advisers.

He is also a partner in a commercial and residential mortgage broking business and is a licenced credit broker under licence no: 166626.

A STAGGERING 40% GROWTH IN SOME INVESTMENT BONDS LEAVES BUILDING SOCIETY RATES FLOUNDERING

Investors who have relied upon Building Society deposit accounts to provide them with an income over the past year hardly need to be told that they have suffered a dramatic reduction in their interest received, now down to around 4.5% p.a. compared with over 12% just two years ago.

Whilst these unfortunates have been struggling, investors who "took the plunge" and invested in insurance company investment bonds have reaped heavy rewards. The top flight managed funds have produced growth of over 40% and even the average performer has made investors' money grow by over 20%.

FOUR TO EIGHT TIMES AS MUCH INCOME AS BUILDING SOCIETIES

This means that the majority of insurance company investment bond investors could have converted this capital growth into an income of four to eight times what they would otherwise have received from a Building Society over the same period.

THE RECESSION IS DEAD – LONG LIVE THE RECOVERY!

Cynics will point out that the recovery is at best patchy and highly fragile. However, the City has a tendency to try to predict the future when fixing the prices of shares. This means that by the time the recovery is fully underway, the share prices will have already risen due to the City's anticipation of this and there will be no room for money to be made simply on the strength of the recovery. The time to invest is therefore before the recovery has fully crystallised. This means now.

TAX-FREE GROWTH AND INCOME

Gains for investors in insurance company investment bonds are free of Capital Gains Tax. They are subject only to the difference between the higher rate and the basic rate of income tax. This means that, for anyone who is a 20% or 25% taxpayer, all the proceeds of an insurance company bond, including income and capital growth are altogether free of tax.

THE NEED FOR PROFESSIONAL INVESTMENT MANAGEMENT

Anyone who has ever sold any shares knows that the price obtained can fluctuate considerably between the time he or she decides to sell and the date the sale actually takes place. The ordinary member of the public cannot possibly know all the factors which will affect the price of a share and therefore know when is it best to buy or sell a share without becoming a professional investor himself. When the professional makes a good buy or sell decision, it is at the uninitiated investors' expense. Insurance company bonds and unit trusts provide cost effective access to professional managers who use their expertise to buy and sell at the right time on your behalf.

THE NEED FOR INDEPENDENT ADVICE

An independent adviser will act in your interests, finding from all the companies available the one or ones which are most suitable to your needs and which have the best investment performance. On the other hand, a representative of only one company can at best only offer the best product from that one company. (Seems obvious, doesn't it?) You cannot tell if that company is the best or the worst for your needs. It always pays to take independent advice.

YOU DON'T HAVE TO SPECULATE TO ACCUMULATE

Making money doesn't have to be a gamble.
There is such a thing as a safe bet. Whatever the size of
your investment. But which option is best?
Which is most profitable? Which one is perfect for you?
For free impartial advice, talk to the experts.
You'll find it all adds up.

YORKSHIRE BUILDING SOCIETY, YORKSHIRE HOUSE, YORKSHIRE DRIVE, BRADFORD BD5 8LJ. TEL: (0274) 740740

FOR FREE IMPARTIAL ADVICE ABOUT MONEY MATTERS

Send to: Yorkshire Building Society, (Customer Information Centre – FAC), Yorkshire House,
Yorkshire Drive, Bradford BD5 8LJ. Please contact me with further details.

Name _____ Address _____ DA/PFA

Postcode _____ Tel _____

It is your right (and your independent financial adviser's obligation) under the Financial Services Act to know whether a fee must be paid or whether the adviser receives a commission for selling financial products. By asking what commission is paid you can be sure that you are being advised to take out financial plans that suit you best and not those with the best commission.

To get a list of independent financial advisers in your area contact IFA Promotion, who will send you a list:

IFA Promotion
28 Greville Street
London EC1N 8SU
Tel: 071-831 4027

Under the Financial Services Act, anyone selling life insurance or investment products has to be tied to one company or group or register as an independent financial adviser.

Financial advisers from the professions are regulated by their recognised professional body: solicitors by the Law Society, chartered accountants by the Institute of Chartered Accountants (of England and Wales) and insurance brokers by the Insurance Brokers Registration Council. Solicitors and accountants charge by the hour, so if you buy a commission-based product from them you can ask for the commission to be deducted from your bill. (See Chapter 10 for useful names and addresses.)

Summary

Remember, it is your money and only you can make the final decision on whether to take someone else's advice. You should check and re-check the recommendations that financial advisers give you. Ask as many questions as you like to satisfy you. Advisers can make mistakes and some are not as good or as professional as others. If you are not sure about their recommendations or you do not trust them, then politely say goodbye and go to another financial adviser. At least then the only thing you have wasted is your time, not your money.

Nor should you be rushed into a decision. A decision can wait. It is not a life or death matter — not for a while, anyway. If, however, you do make the wrong decision in your view and are not happy with the advice given, then the Financial Services Act does stipulate that you are allowed a 'cooling-off' period of 14 days for certain types of investment including life insurance, pensions and unit trusts. This enables you to cancel the contract with no loss of money.

As a last resort you can claim compensation from the Investors Compensation Scheme if you lose money because you are wrongly advised, someone runs off with your money or the firm you are investing in is declared bankrupt. However, you will not be compensated for poor performance or market losses.

How to complain effectively and get your money back

When the Financial Services Act was introduced in 1988, a complaints and compensation system was set up to bail out investors if the worst happened and to ensure that regulated firms did not break the rules set up to protect investors.

The chief regulatory authority is the Securities and Investments Board (SIB). Each of the sub-regulators has its own complaints and compensation arrangements.

However, they will not make awards if you are left worse off just because the stock market falls. Your loss has to be because of bad advice, incompetence or bad administration.

FIMBRA

The Financial Intermediaries and Brokers Regulatory Authority — which is merging with LAUTRO to form the PIA (Personal Investment Authority) — has a complaints scheme run by the Chartered Institute of Arbitrators. The maximum payout is £50,000.

FIMBRA
Hertsmere House
Hertsmere Road
London E14 4AB
Tel: 071-538 8860

PIAS (The Personal Insurance
  Arbitration Service)
Chartered Institute of Arbitrators
24 Angel Gate
City Road
London EC1V 2RS
Tel: 071-837 4483

LAUTRO

The Life Assurance and Unit Trust Regulatory Organisation regulates insurance and unit trust companies. It is to merge with FIMBRA to form the PIA. LAUTRO uses the Insurance Ombudsman and the

Investment Ombudsman to deal with complaints about its members.

LAUTRO Complaints Department
Canterbury House
2–6 Sydenham Road
Croydon
Surrey CRO 9XE
Tel: 081-686 9309

IMRO

The Investment Managers' Regulatory Authority runs a complaints scheme through the Investment Ombudsman, who can make awards of up to £100,000.

Contact: IMRO
Broadwalk House
5 Appold Street
London EC2A 2LL
Tel: 071-628 6022

SFA

The Securities and Futures Authority regulates stockbrokers and dealers in futures and options. Its Consumer Arbitration Scheme can pay out up to £50,000 in compensation. There is a registration fee of £10.

SFA
Stock Exchange Buildings
12 Old Broad Street
London EC2N 1EQ
Tel: 071-378 9000

Other financial advisers are regulated by what are known as Recognised Professional Bodies (RPB). These include those described below.

IBRC

The Insurance Brokers Registration Council has a membership of around 4100 insurance brokers at any one time. It handles complaints from the public against member insurance brokers. The IBRC can strike off a broker and support a member of the public through a Grants Fund if a broker is taken to court and cannot pay.

The Insurance Brokers Registration Council
15 St Helen's Place
London EC3A 6DE
Tel: 071-588 4387

ICAEW

The Institute of Chartered Accountants in England and Wales regulates chartered accountants who have to apply to become an authorised provider of financial services and investment business (see Chapter 10 for the address of the Institute of Chartered Accountants of Scotland).

The Institute of Chartered Accountants in England and Wales
PO Box 433
Chartered Accountants Hall
Moorgate Place
London EC2P 2BJ
Tel: 071-628 7060

Law Society

The Law Society is the organisation that controls the activities and behaviour of solicitors in England and Wales and administers the Legal Aid Scheme. It also regulates solicitors who are involved in investment business (see Chapter 10 for the addresses of the Law Societies of Scotland and Northern Ireland).

Solicitors' dealings in financial services fall into two distinct categories: discrete and non-discrete business. Discrete business is where they offer their own advice on financial matters; non-discrete business is where they offer financial products from a third party, but no personal advice. Up to 7000 out of the 10,000 members of the Law Society are authorised to conduct investment business by SIB. Check which ones are authorised before signing anything.

The Law Society
113 Chancery Lane
London WC2A 1PL
Tel: 071-242 1222

Chartered Association of Certified Accountants

ACCA monitors and regulates its members and investigates complaints from the public against members who are registered with SIB to provide investment advice.

ACCA
29 Lincoln's Inn Fields
London WC2A 3EE
Tel: 071-396 5700

Institute of Actuaries

The Institute of Actuaries is the body that represents actuaries who are qualified to assess and evaluate risks. They are key figures who have statutory obligations to ensure that a policy or fund remains financially viable. The body is also responsible for policing its members' work if it receives complaints.

The Institute of Actuaries
Staples Inn Hall
High Holborn
London WC1V 7QJ
Tel: 071-242 0106

Some firms may not need authorisation. Mortgages do not come under the scope of the Financial Services Act, nor do bank deposits or savings as they are not classed as long-term investments.

Investment companies that go bust — who to claim compensation from

The Investors' Compensation Scheme was set up to protect people who lose money through an investment firm which then goes bust. It will refund the first £30,000 of your investment, plus 90 per cent of the next £20,000 — making a maximum pay out of £48,000. Contact:

The Securities and Investments Board
Gavrelle House
2–14 Bunhill Row
London EC1Y 8RA
Tel: 071-638 1240

The Bank of England runs a Deposit Protection Scheme which will pay out a maximum of £15,000 if a bank goes under: this is 75 per cent of up to £20,000. Contact:

The Bank of England
Threadneedle Street
London EC2R 8AH
Tel: 071-601 4444

Consumers' main protection regarding building societies is under the 1986 Building Societies Act. In the unlikely event of a building society going bust, as a last resort there is a compensation scheme, the Investor Protection Scheme, which will pay out a maximum of £18,000 — this is 90 per cent of £20,000, or 90 per cent of £40,000 if it is a joint account. Contact:

The Building Societies Commission
15 Great Marlborough Street
London W1V 2AX
Tel: 071-437 9992

If an insurance company fails, you can claim up to 90 per cent of the value of your policy in the case of compulsory policies — only employers' liability — and 100 per cent on non-compulsory policies — including house contents, buildings insurance, travel insurance and personal accident policies. Contact:

The Policy Holders Protection Board
51 Gresham Street
London EC2V 7HQ
Tel: 071-600 3333

If you are a victim of a car accident with a hit-and-run driver or where there is no proper third-party insurance, you can try to get redress and the whole matter sorted out through the help of the Motor Insurers' Bureau — a body set up by insurance companies. Contact:

The Motor Insurers' Bureau
152 Silbury Boulevard
Central Milton Keynes
MK9 1NB
Tel: 0908 240000

Where to complain

Don't waste your money on expensive legal fees, if you can possibly avoid it. Go to an ombudsman to get your complaint dealt with for free. You must first approach the head office of the company that you have a problem with. If you remain dissatisfied with the way the matter has been dealt with then as soon as you can (usually within three to six months of the last correspondence you have had with the company you think is at fault — but check beforehand) you should raise the matter with an ombudsman.

Fortunately, the services of an ombudsman and other complaints bureaux are normally free of charge, so you don't have spend vast sums of money fighting a company through the courts, and they may award you compensation of up to £100,000.

Ombudsmen are independent referees who will blow the whistle if savers and investors are treated unfairly.

Banks

The Banking Ombudsman will deal with complaints about the banks. The scheme covers all the main UK high street banks and their subsidiaries.

The Banking Ombudsman
70 Gray's Inn Road
London WC1X 8NB
Tel: 071-404 9944

Building societies

The Building Societies Ombudsman can handle grievances about mortgages, savings, cheques and cashpoint machines.

The Building Societies Ombudsman
Grosvenor Gardens House
35–37 Grosvenor Gardens
London SW1X 7AW
Tel: 071-931 0044

Estate agents

The Corporate Estate Agents Ombudsman deals with complaints from the public who have problems with registered estate agents.

Corporate Estate Agents Ombudsman
PO Box 1114
Salisbury
Wilts
SP1 1YQ
Tel: 0722 333306

Insurance

The Insurance Ombudsman covers most UK insurance companies. As well as general insurance such as household or motor, life assurance complaints are handled.

Any complaints against a Lloyd's of London syndicate should first be referred to the Lloyd's Consumer Advice Department. Thereafter they can be passed onto the Insurance Ombudsman, as Lloyd's motor syndicates are members. The Insurance Ombudsman has absorbed the former Unit Trust Ombudsman's functions.

The Insurance Ombudsman
City Gate One
135 Park Street London SE1 9EA
Tel: 071-928 4488

Investments

The Investment Ombudsman largely covers the members of IMRO, but also some unit trust companies.

The Investment Ombudsman
6 Fredericks Place
London EC2R 8BJ
Tel: 071-796 3065

Solicitors

The Legal Services Ombudsman oversees the handling of complaints against solicitors, barristers and licensed conveyancers for negligence, poor service and so on.

The Legal Services Ombudsman
22 Oxford Court

Oxford Street
Manchester M2 3WQ
Tel: 061-236 9532

Pensions

The Pensions Ombudsman can deal with both company and personal
pension problems — maladministration by trustees or managers of
occupational or personal pension schemes. There is no limit on compensation that can be awarded. People usually go first to OPAS
(Occupational Pensions Advisory Service), a voluntary service which
offers experts to sort out problems before referral to the Pensions
Ombudsman.

The Pensions Ombudsman
11 Belgrave Road
London SW1V 1RB
Tel: 071-834 9144

OPAS
11 Belgrave Road
London SW1V 1RB
Tel: 071-834 9144

The Solicitors Complaints Bureau deals with complaints against
solicitors from members of the public who want compensation for negligence and inadequate service. The SCB has the power to force a
solicitor to pay a client up to £1000 for any financial loss, serious
inconvenience or distress caused by inadequate service.

The SCB also deals with claims about overcharging for work done.
A lot of bills come in higher than the solicitor's original estimate.

Solicitors Complaints Bureau
Victoria Court
8 Dormer House
Leamington Spa
Warwicks CV32 5AE
Tel: 0926 820082

10
Sources of further information

Association of British Insurers (ABI)
51 Gresham Street
London EC1V 7HQ
Tel: 071-600 3333

Association of British Credit Unions
Unit 305
339 Kensington Lane
London SE11 5QY
Tel: 071-582 2626

Association of Investment Trust
  Companies (AITC)
Park House
6th Floor
16 Finsbury Circus
London EC2M 7JJ
Tel: 071-588 5347

Association of Unit Trusts Investment
  Funds (AUTIF) (formerly the Unit
  Trust Association)
65 Kingsway
London WC2B 6TD
Tel: 071-831 0898

Bank of England
Threadneedle Street
London EC2R 8AH
Tel: 071-601 4444

Banking Information Services
10 Lombard Street
London EC3V 9AP
Tel: 071-626 8486

Banking Ombudsman
70 Gray's Inn Road
London WC1X 8NB
Tel: 071-404 9944

Bankruptcy Association of Great
  Britain and Ireland
4 Johnson Close
Lancaster LA1 5EU
Tel: 0482 658701

British Insurance and Investment
  Brokers Association (BIIBA)
BIIBA House
14 Bevis Marks
London EC3A 7NT
Tel: 071-623 9043

Building Societies Association (BSA)
3 Savile Row
London W1X 1AF
Tel: 071-437 0655

Building Societies Commission
15 Great Marlborough Street
London W1V 2AX
Tel: 071-437 9992

Building Societies Ombudsman
Grosvenor Gardens House
35–37 Grosvenor Gardens
London SW1X 7AW
Tel: 071-931 0044

Chartered Association of Certified
Accountants (ACCA)
29 Lincoln's Inn Fields
London WC2A 3EE
Tel: 071-396 5700

Chartered Institute of Arbitrators
24 Angel Gate
City Road
London EC1V 2RS
Tel: 071-837 4483

Citizens Advice Bureaux Scotland
26 George Square
Edinburgh EH8 9LD
Tel: 031-667 0156

Consumers Association
2 Marylebone Road
London NW1 4DX1
Tel: 071-486 5544

Council for Licensed Conveyancers
16 Glebe Road
Chelmsford
Essex CM1 1QG
Tel: 0245 349599

Council of Mortgage Lenders (CML)
(see entry for Building Societies
Association)

Corporate Estate Agents Ombudsman
PO Box 1114
Salisbury
Wiltshire SP1 1YQ
Tel: 0722 333306

Corporation of Professional Loss
Assessors
83 Crawford Street
London W1H 2AB
Tel: 071-724 9693

Department of Social Security (DSS)
Richmond House
79 Whitehall

London SW1A 2NS
Public Enquiry Office — 071-210 5983
— Benefit Equiry Line — 0800 882200
(Open 9am–4.30pm, Monday to
Friday)
— Social Security Freelance Line —
0800 666555
(Open 9am–4.30pm, Monday to
Friday)

Federation of Independent Advice
Centres
13 Stockwell Road
London SW9 9AU
Tel: 071-274 1839

Financial Intermediaries, Managers
and Brokers Regulatory
Association (FIMBRA)
Hertsmere House
Hertsmere Road
London E14 4AB
Tel: 071-538 8860

IFA Promotion
28 Greville Street
London EC1N 8SU
Tel: 071-831 4027
— IFA Consumer Hotline — 0483
461461

Incorporated Society of Valuers and
Auctioneers (ISVA)
3 Cadogan Gate
London SW1X OAP
Tel: 071-235 2282

Inland Revenue (IR)
Somerset House
The Strand
London WC1R 1LB
Tel: 071-438 6622
— Tax Enquiry Line — 071-438 6420

Institute of Actuaries
Staples Inn Hall
High Holborn
London WC1V 7QJ
Tel: 071-242 0106

Institute of Chartered Accountants in
England & Wales (ICAEW)
PO Box 433
Chartered Accountants Hall
Moorgate Place
London EC2P 2BJ
Tel: 071-628 7060

Institute of Chartered Accountants of
Scotland
27 Queen Street
Edinburgh EH2 1LA
Tel: 031-225 5673

Institute of Insurance Brokers (IIB)
Higham Business Centre
Midland Road
Higham Ferrers
Northhampton NN9 8DW
Tel: 0933 410003

Institute of Taxation
12 Upper Belgrave Street
London SW1X 8BA
Tel: 071-235 9381

Insurance Brokers Registration
Council (IBRC)
15 St Helens Place
London EC3A 6DE
Tel: 071-588 4387

Insurance Ombudsman
City Gate One
135 Park Street
London SE1 9EA
Tel: 071-928 4488

Investment Management Regulatory
Organisation (IMRO)
Broadwalk House
5 Appold Street
London EC2A 2LL
Tel: 071-628 6022

Investment Ombudsman
6 Fredericks Place
London EC2R 8BJ
Tel: 071-796 3065

Land Registry
32 Lincoln's Inn Fields
London WC2A 3PH
Tel: 071-917 8888

Law Centres Federation
Duchess House
18–19 Warren Street
London W1P 5DB
Tel: 071-387 8570

Law Society
113 Chancery Lane
London WC2A 1PL
Tel: 071-242 1222

Law Society of Northern Ireland
Law Society House
98 Victoria Street
Belfast BT1 3JZ
Tel: 0232 231614

Law Society of Scotland
26 Drumsheugh Gardens
Edinburgh EH3 7YR
Tel: 031-226 7411

Legal Services Ombudsman
22 Oxford Court
Oxford Street
Manchester M2 3WQ
Tel: 061-236 9532

Life Assurance and Unit Trust
  Regulatory Organisation (LAUTRO)
Centre Point
103 New Oxford Street
London WC1A 1QH
Tel: 071-379 0444

Life Insurance Association (LIA)
Citadel House
Station Approach
Chorleywood
Herts WD3 5PS
Tel: 092328 5333

London International Financial
  Futures and Options Exchange
  (LIFFE)
Cannon Bridge
London EC4R 3XX
Tel: 071-623 0444

Motor Insurers' Bureau (MIB)
152 Silbury Boulevard
Central Milton Keynes MK9 1NB
Tel: 0908 240000

National Association of Citizens
  Advice Bureaux (NACAB)
Myddeleton House
115–123 Pentonville Road
London N1 9LZ
Tel: 071-833 2181
– General Enquiry Line: 081-459
  2780 (10am-4pm)
– National Debtline: 021-359 8501

National Association of Estate Agents
  (NAEA)
21 Jury Street
Warwick CV34 4EW
Tel: 0926 496800

National Consumer Council (NCC)
20 Grosvenor Gardens
London SW1W OBD
Tel: 071-730 3469

Occupational Pensions Advisory
  Service (OPAS)
11 Belgrave Road
London SW1V 1RB
Tel: 071-233 8080

Office of Fair Trading (OFT)
Field House
15–25 Bream's Buildings
London EC4N 5BH
Tel: 071-242 2858

Pensions Ombudsman
11 Belgrave Road
London SW1V 1RB
Tel: 071-834 9144

Personal Insurance Arbitration
  Service (PIAS)
(See entry for Chartered Institute of
  Arbitration for full address)

Personal Investment Association (PIA)
3/4 Royal Exchange Buildings
London EC3V 3NL
Tel: 071-929 0072

Policy Holders Protection Board
51 Gresham Street
London EC2V 7HQ
Tel: 071-600 3333

Principal Probate Registry
Somerset House
The Strand
London WC2A 2LL
Tel: 071-936 6939

Probate Registry (Scotland)
HM Commissary Office
Sheriff Court House
16 Northbank Street
Lawn Market
Edinburgh EH1 2NS
Tel: 031-226 7181

Registry of Friendly Societies
15 Great Marlborough Street
London W1V 2AX
Tel: 071-437 9992

Royal Institution of Chartered
 Surveyors (RICS)
12 Great George Street
Parliament Square
London SW1P 3AD
Tel: 071-222 7000

The Securities and Futures Authority
12 Old Broad Street
London EC2N 1EQ
Tel: 071-378 9000

Securities and Investments Board
 (SIB)
Gavrelle House
2–14 Bunhill Row
London EC1Y 8RA
Tel: 071-638 1240

Solicitors Complaints Bureau
Victoria Court
8 Dormer House
Leamington Spa
Warwicks CV32 5AE
Tel: 0926 820082

Solicitors' Family Law Association
PO Box 302
Keston
Kent BR2 6E2
Tel: 0689 850227

Index

Index of Advertisers